Pearls of the Peace Land

by ZoRe

Editing: Kristin M Grippo
Graphic Design: Ali Tajik

Aum Twameva Sakshat Shri Ganesha
Sakshat Shri Adi Shakti Mataji
Shri Nirmala Devyai Namo Namaha

Sumuka Ekadanta Kapila Gaja karnaka
Lambodara Vikata Vighna nasha
Ganadhipa Dhumra ketu
Ganadhyaksha Bala chandra Gajanana

Special thanks to:

My husband Steven
My parents
Lavanya Rao Nicola
Nidhi Singh
And all the people of this journey…

Contents

Foreword

Since our marriage that began in the USA, the journey of understanding, growing, and integrating has been tremendous. This book exemplifies this in so many ways. Of course, the story starts in Iran and continues in Italy, but the pieces come together in the USA, the binding force is the Sahaja marriage that starts and continues to be true to its core of growth in the Self.

Over the years of our marriage since 2005, the hills and valleys have been many. Through it all has been the faith in our true Selves and the courage to move forward one pearl at a time in the present moment of truth, love and compassion.

This is a book about our frailties and illusions as well as our strengths and aspirations. Most importantly, this is a book that ultimately captures the message of arriving and being grateful to our true Self.

So the journey is to be enjoyed …

- *Steven Marchitelli*

Preface

The present moment is the real strand of pearls in the Goddess' hands. She helped me to put together the past and the future, from my ancestral influences to my futuristic projections, to the now; stringing the pearls one by one, together with poems, fables, and memories, to create this one true Peace Land. Today, I believe more than ever that "God is the doer and enjoyer; that I do nothing." I move forward with gratitude and peace in my heart.

After the big bang and the creation of this world, each human being is a masterpiece once they become aware of their real value. As a seeker of truth, I went through a lot in my childhood in Iran, as well as, in my young age in Italy. And, as an older adult woman in the USA, I went through a culmination of rough times to finally learn about myself and life as a precious gift. I believe today that life is something between tragedies and hopes, desperations and good wishes, a killing duality that teaches you only one precious thing: be grateful and go beyond!

- *ZoRe*

A Prayer

Mother, when I look at your photo, I see where you are taking me... You take me to your Divine dimension, where I am part of you!

I see everything around me as it is You. You are the creator of all and you with your immense grace let me be one of your cells.

Mother, I can experience only with you my existence of a universal being; with each of your gestures everything moves, some close, some far, and some with you. You are the cosmic extension and expansion.

Mother Thank you for letting us be part of this Divine experience; of looking at everything in the greater picture, of not being entangled in our little world.

Mother because of you, we have no fear of death, because we know that you are always with us. Oh dear Sandra Karuna, Thank You!

Creation
Based on the words of H.H. Shri Mataji Nirmala Devi

Once upon a time there was a very divine darkness and silent existence. It was going in this way for a very long time, for an eternity.

The Shakti, the power of God, or the female aspect of the divine, felt the desire of Her consort for a change. In Her own existence, She was aware that the change would be very dramatic. Out of love for Her consort Shiva, and to create a new life, She had to separate Herself from Him and to stand out of their orbit of unison. In an evolutionary pulsation, the Big Bang transpired, upon which the first Divine sound echoed in the Universe: AUM. An all-powerful force, thus expressing their everlasting love, ended the eternal darkness.

To keep Shiva always in Her heart, She ensured that in every small and big aspect that She created, there was the subtle essence of Shiva's primordial presence. In order to reflect the uniqueness of His qualities, She used a myriad of mirrors. She first began with dividing Herself into three branches. These branches emerged out of the same source and are called channels. Each represented Shiva's main qualities: his primordial existence, his awareness (Sat), his Knowledge (Chit), and the absolute joy of union (Ananda).

Shakti then designated a feminine deity for each of

the three channels: Maha Lakshmi, Maha Saraswati, and Maha Kali. Also, with a vision to bring more balance, She additionally assigned three Divine deity couples: Shri Lakshmi and Shri Vishnu, Shri Brahma Deva and Shri Saraswati, and Shri Shiva and Shri Parvati. Their task was to protect and evolve the channels and chakras where they were seated. The foundation of all Her creations was love for the great spirit of Shiva, God almighty and his children.

Yet She felt some incompleteness in the process of Her own creation. A strong desire occurred upon Her to create something from Her own Self, someone who was a symbol of Herself. The motherly desire of Her heart perspired through Her skin as sweat. It is this very perspiration, fragrant and holy, She used to create an idol of the son that She aspired for. She poured life into this idol and called him Ganesha. She made him as the embodiment of wisdom and chastity. And Ganesha in return surrendered his innate faith and dedication towards His holy Mother. She sang and played beautiful melodies to Her beloved Ganesha, teaching him divine art and knowledge. “I bestow upon you the pure knowledge and teach you the divine principles, my darling.” She declared to her divine child.

The powers and blessings of Ganesha were so abundant that the Devi, the Queen of the Godland, did not need an infantry of Her own anymore to guard and protect Her against the numerous enemies. Ganesha alone was capable of holding off an entire army himself, just like an obedient and trustworthy son. He was the fragrance of his Mother, and at the same time, a strong Ganapati who later on became a militia commander, the "Chief of all the Ganas."

Once divine love and its purity was established, Shiva granted Her the freedom of the whole of creation at every level, from celestial to mundane, and the task to govern creation was also conferred upon Her. The joy of the first child was so immense that She created even more beautiful and surprising creatures to amuse Her consort. And while Her consort was relaxing, watching Her play as the only spectator, She was working tirelessly, emanating a powerful pulsing consciousness from Her own being into each aspect of Her creation: universes after universes. With Her Love for the children of earth, She started creating life. Thus began the pulsation of life on earth which triggered an evolution. The goal of all this was to become a perfect mirror of Shiva: the pure spirit.

Enthusiastic about Her results, one day She felt that it was time for Her grown-up, beloved son to meet his Father. She took Ganesha's hand in Hers, guiding him to the chamber of his Father. "Stay here my child; you are going to have a meeting with your Father, Lord Shiva." Ganesha hesitated; a bitter taste from past memories was holding him back (1). The Devi, his Mother, could sense the turmoil of Her son and so stayed with him at the door to calm him down by singing the melodies that were familiar to his ears. Lord Shiva, as always, was still sitting in a lotus position and witnessing everything around him with no reaction. In his chamber, strange looking people had gathered; from ugly demons with their dark shadows to beautiful angels with their bright crystal glows. Frightened by the chamber's atmosphere, Ganesha couldn't feel his own gravity and started to step back.

His Father, Lord Shiva, had come closer, trying to take his hand with a soft rhythmic dance to convince him to be in a safe place: A dance for the destruction of darkness (*Tandav*), a dance to protect innocence and to nourish peace. Ganesha started to feel that rhythm in his heart and followed his Father's steps. For an eternity they danced and danced until there was finally the light of truth, awareness, and joy.

Outside the chamber of Lord Shiva, in the center of the universe, Mother Devi was at war with the ignorant dark forces of deep down worlds, which could not bear upon the magnificent dance of Shiva and Ganesha in unison. In the eternal love that the Devi held for Her own creation, She defeated the dark forces by devouring them with the same dance of destruction. Eventually the light of truth, awareness and joy emerged and peace was restored upon the entire land of Gods.

"Dance my child, dance!" Shakti proclaimed. And in this way, She could show Lord Shiva her love and Her power at the same time. Finally, in this new dimension of pervading light and sovereignty, they could play as an eternal family. And from their unison of trinity emerged the creation of earth through the powers of the Virata (2). Once the essence of this material world was stabilized with elements, nature, and animals, She finally designed humans as reflectors of Godliness on earth. Thus the Peace Land was created!

Humans were born from the breath of life and with this great opportunity; humans started the evolutionary journey of becoming the pure Spirit. Now it was upon them to find their way and to discover meaning for their purpose on earth. For their Holy Mother also gave them freedom to choose. Therefore, it was their chance to manifest their purpose and understand the subtle energy they received.

Yet in the course of their evolutionary growth, human beings slowly started losing their innocence to ignorance, thus falling prey to greed, ego, and jealousies. The dark powers were attempting to take control over the earth. Therefore, it was about time for the Devi to bring a great warrior to earth, one who could kindle the inner light and save the seekers from death and ignorance. She, the Mother, had to protect Her children on earth.

In the heavenly abode, Ganesha could sense the pain of his Mother, the Goddess. He was determined to support his Mother. Ganesha thus shared with Mother Devi his intention of sacrificing his own very subtle body to free the human mind from the darkness of ignorance. "Mother, I want to prove my gratitude to You and Father. Let me please participate in Your creation process and play a drama that will lead your children on earth into a new stage of awareness. Only through forgiveness, they will be able to embrace the recognition of Eternity!"

"The spirit is eternal," She whispered in contemplation, confirming his statement and accepting his will, and the destiny was fulfilled immediately. "Oh my dear Son, you've reached your goal of resurrecting humans in their awareness. Your Father is pleased with your decision. So, now go and join your Father. (3)"

With the permission of Devi and his Father, he decided to rise up into his alpha and omega state in order to emanate subtle vibrations. He thus had to take his birth in a physical body and by doing that, he was transformed into his full expression: Christ, the Lord! It was only with this new form and avatar that he could sustain human awareness and human evolution. His pure desire to rise and to ascend mankind to the dimension of divinity was so impressive that a golden gate spontaneously opened, and humans' hearts and minds were united. Shiva, with deep affection toward his Son, proudly gazed and smiled. Ganesha was born in a new avatar, as the epitome of vibrations, with the name of Jesu (Jesus).

Moved by both the pure love of the Holy Mother and the dedication of his son for protecting humanity on earth, Shiva asked the supreme Devi to take a seat on His head as a golden crown in eternal joy. In this new form of union with Shiva, She was able to protect Her son Ganesha, and all Her other creations forever.

From that day forth, an everlasting motherly love flows from the human fontanel bone. Its subtle, yet divine totality fills our pores with everlasting auspiciousness. For this reason, humans are able to connect directly with God. Humans are able to achieve the final purpose: to become the mirror reflecting Father Shiva. No more states of confusion or darkness. Instead, a penetrating light of purity and divine love is flowing out into existence. And then after, the free will of humanity will be imploded into the pure desire of God.

(1) This refers to the story in which Lord Shiva, not recognizing Ganesha, cut off His head.

(2) Virat is the 11th incarnation of Shri Vishnu, the deity of Evolutionary process. Virat is the brain of God Almighty, located in the central nervous system of all human beings which evolves by transformation of Vishnu into Krishna and ultimately in Virat (God's Brain).

(3) This refers to the Statue of Piety of Michelangelo in which the hand of Mother Mary, in contemplation, indicates the path of freedom and a soft smile of Christ with open mouth shows his satisfaction of what he had accomplished.

Aum Twamewa Sakshat
Shri Hazrate Ali-Fatemeh Sakshat Shri
Brahmadeva-Saraswati Sakshat Shri
Adi Shakti Mataji
Shri Nirmala Devyai Namo Namaha

Aum Twamewa Sakshat
Shri Adi Guru Dattatreya Sakshat Shri
Adi Shakti Mataji
Shri Nirmala Devyai Namo Namaha

The Silk Thread

God places a silk thread in your hand and says to you, "If you want to see me, follow this thread." With just the desire to see him, you follow that long silky thread. You start an unknown trip to an unknown destination.

You walk and walk until you start to feel tired. You want to stop somewhere to have some water and something to eat. In that unknown desert, it looks impossible, but all of a sudden you find in front of you a caravansary. An ancient place created for travelers to stay appears to you like a mirage.

You can feel a cool breeze coming from inside as soon as you arrive at its threshold. Pausing on the cool heavy stone floor, covered with a beautiful Persian rug, you slowly move toward a turquoise pond to refresh your feet in its canal. Breathing deep into your lungs, you can feel the freshness of the air mix with the water vapor. You take advantage of the fresh running water and wash your face. Everything emanates of joy and warmth at the same time. The harmonious dance of goldfish in the water captures your eyes and you feel lost in that beauty.

You let water run on your arms and head, getting ready for *namaz*, your daily prayer to God almighty. You go toward the main hall, passing through *ghahve khane* (a coffee shop), stepping up on a large, tall, well-curved stone; nobody is there but you.

You sit and wait. There are long reddish curtains that divide the courtyard from the hall. They give a vitality and readiness to face life, creating a vivid contrast with the turquoise of the pond. The movement of the fountain and the gray stones of the floor invite you to stay still and calm.

Just then, a man with a yellow shawl around his waist enters. He wears a long white tunic and pants of the same color. He leaves his loose old boots of cotton at the foot of the steps, rushing to offer you a soft cotton towel. You take it with a sense of gratitude, and dry your hands and face with it. You feel the urge to ask, "Where am I?"

Hassan Agha (1), this huge and strong man, invites you to sit and replies, "Yazd Baba!"

His soft voice assures you and you sit, leaning into huge, colorful cushions. Hassan Agha places hot tea in a transparent glass in front of you and invites you to enjoy it. The aroma of that bergamot tea is astonishing. He offers another small tray with different glass bowls of hard sugar, candies, and baklava.

In all these simple offers, you feel the flow of love and attention toward you. Even the earth, under those huge cushions, is taking away a burden from you. You feel at home! You raise your head with a sense of gratitude in your heart and notice the huge dome of the ceiling, made of mud and straw, with white inserts of gypsum. All together this creates a magnificent and spiritual atmosphere. You feel no need to sweeten your black tea. In surrender and trust, you close your eyes and listen to Hassan Agha narrate the story of Iran, the land of ancient Persia …

(1) Hassan is one of the sons of Imam Ali and Fatimah. He is also the reincarnation of Archangel Gabriel. His outfit is symbolically yellow, representing the right channel. His role is to announce the truth and to give knowledge.

Finding My Way in Her Peace Land

I grew up in the very distant country of Iran. At the age of five, I lost my sweet great-grandmother and later on my grandfather. From these two lost, I learned that dear people around me could die. I couldn't get it, why should there be such bad things in the world?

A few years later, I was mesmerized by a soccer game in the dusty streets of my neighborhood. I watched, absorbed in the fascinating efforts of young boys running behind a white ball, creating such an enormous amount of dust as if to almost make themselves invisible. I could taste deeper and deeper in my mouth and throat the raising soil of that humble playground as the play ran like a movie in front of my eyes. Considering that in those times no girl was authorized to play soccer, for me, watching the game was in some ways an act of disobedience.

As I watched in that total engagement, I was unaware of a moto heading straight toward me with no chance of escape. It crashed into me, pushing me into a huge stone that had been substituting as a goal post. I felt a strong pain rushing inside my body, but did not cry or shout. Despite seeing my twisted leg, feeling the pain sulking inside my stomach, I somehow felt amused. Just then I had been pushed into real life. I tried to stand up, but something was wrong: one of my legs couldn't hold me. In fact, my tiny right leg had been broken. The moto rider picked me up and took me home. All the way I was calm and sober in giving the address and showing the man the way.

Once I arrived home, I got a different picture of what had just happened. My mother was screaming, shedding lots of tears: *How?! Why? She could have been killed! She could be* dead*!* The word *dead* echoed in my head. It was then that I understood that it can come to everyone, this dreadful thing, even through something as innocent as watching a soccer match. I silently swore to my invisible enemy that I was not afraid of it, that I was the courageous daughter/soldier of my father!

In the weeks that followed, naturally, everyone wanted to express themselves by writing or painting something on my cast, like little children in front of a white board today at school. I enjoyed the colors and messages on my cast until it was removed, after two months. The moment I felt the breeze of my liberated leg was so amusing! The hairs that had grown on my tiny leg would catch the wind and make me laugh. With that laughter, I was praising life over death.

As I grew, I learned that I was the first child of the third generation. That meant that I was to bear a large burden of responsibility by taking care of others, from my younger siblings to my elderly grandparents. I was the recipient of all kinds of attention from my family. Uncles and aunts from both sides wanted me to be or to do *something*: Be a good student, a good musician, a good girl. In addition, everyone had opinions about *how* I should do things: How to dress, speak, even how to play!

Dancing was the only time that I felt free to fly in my imagination. I could soar with the rhythm of my uncle's violin, jumping high and dropping down low. The mysterious melody coming from those strings would create the most joyful feelings and took me far from the small pressing world around her. In my imagination, I performed for invisible audiences for hours. The love between my uncle and I had a magic nature; I could feel him beyond his words in those melodies. He dedicated a special song to me, which summarized my feelings for him and the music. The was called Zohreh, The Celestial Bride.

While some family members had the intention of embarrassing me over such a grand title, I knew about the love behind my artist-uncle's melody, and felt honored. Soon, people around me began to call me "Celestial Bride," dropping my name.

Unfortunately, this designation did not bring with it a lighter life, but rather, continued expectations. I was still caring for everybody. My mother's side of the family was so different from my father's. They were two extreme opposites; on one side came the request for an artist and on the other side a rebel woman. I had to move between my mother's side that had me seeking aesthetic patterns in natural and artificial things, to my father's side of studying socio- economic and political resolutions.

Meanwhile, while my one uncle was passionately playing violin in a life of freedom, I had another uncle that was a political prisoner, consuming boiled nails in water to survive the lack of sun in his little dark prison cell. My father was lucky to have escaped the fate of his companions, considering that all his five brothers and his only sister were activists against the government. These intellectuals could talk about the root of an onion for hours, or how they were considered like beetles in the eyes of regime. They were courageous and ready to sacrifice everything, including their lives, for the sake of freedom of their country, but so disconnected with the whole and with the Divine.

While I was privy to these in-depth ruminations, on the other side, I was witnessing all kinds of light love stories. Between the two, as a teenage activist, I liked my father's ideas and programs better. I thought that this type of attitude would help me to survive the tough waves and not be lost between reality and ideals. This side of the family felt a safer island to land, where I could translate my emotions into rational mental concepts. In this way, I started to become more and more logical and less and less joyful.

* * *

Many years later, as an adult, I was introduced to a book, *The New Modern Era,* written by Shri Mataji Nirmala Devi. It was there that I received all of the answers and even the resolution for the world's problems. All those complicated political ideas of my dad's party that I had been studying for years were now easy tasks to deal with. I was amazed and at the same time a bit upset about the time I wasted. There were explanations for every situation of each country and continent and the way to uplift all of them.

A few months after my self-realization, I noticed that in the presence of Shri Mataji, I became so joyful, clapping and laughing like I was a little child. I so much desired that these cherished feelings stay with me forever that I began to ask Shri Mataji in my meditation to give me the same joy as I was feeling in Her presence. Months later, on Mother's Day, when all yogis in Cabella went to visit Mother for the occasion, Shri Mataji asked me, "Are you in joy?" In the moment I just nodded my head "Yes." Later on though, I recognized the vastness of the drama: "She can hear me in my meditations!" In that moment I was overcome with tears at the feeling of connection with the infinite and my own sense of freedom. Mother's voice was echoing in my head again and again: *Are you in joy?*

A Resurrecting Dance

I was dancing on the shore, yes, I was. Watching my oblique shadow moving with me was spectacular. I pretended to fly like a pelican, swinging my wings and skimming the air. I loved to watch my shadow become so smooth and artistic on that shore.

I know that day I was a new person. I had a dream the night before: In the dream it was the night of Halloween. I was in the middle of a confusion, with lots of people around me. I saw both my deceased uncles. One of them was coming toward me and he was upset; I felt so much love for him. I understood that he was my angry side. He was the uncle I had spent most of my childhood with. We both loved spending time in nature. He was a free man innately, even though he had to spend almost twenty years of his life in prison and be tortured because of his beliefs. Nature for him was a best friend. He finished his imprisonment by the Shah, but never got rid of his own prison of anger and resentment.

Then I saw another uncle from my mother's side. He was a refined artist. He died of a heart attack in the period of revolution, when they tried to shut down his music class, breaking all his musical instruments. He was always so generous and kind with everybody and especially with me. In my dream he brought sweets and fruits for us to share, but it was clear that he wasn't a happy person. Even if he tried to be transparent in giving things, he was always hiding his unhappiness. I asked my mother, in the dream, if I could give him his realization and my mother replied, "Not now, maybe tomorrow." I understood that I had to leave for university and around me as usual was confusion: books and mats everywhere. I went out with people who came to see me from the rooftops. At that moment I noticed that we were in the house of Shri Mataji in Genova. I guided people from the roof of her house down to our destination. I understood then the meaning of this dream. In facing my two dear uncles, I learned that before helping others, I had to go beyond my own anger and dissatisfaction.

The next morning, I felt like I was in a comfortable nest, abandoning all man-made disciplines, rituals, and techniques in favor of spontaneity. I knew that to get rid of all the structures and conditionings takes time, and that it may not happen in my lifetime. I felt the best way to spread Her vision, especially in the USA, was through the power of Virata (1) and collective consciousness, and for that I should become very humble and graceful.

(1)

(1) Virat is the 11th incarnation of Shri Vishnu, the deity of Evolutionary process. He is the brain of God Almighty, located in the central nervous system of all human beings.

Aum Twamewa Sakshat Shri Hazrat
Fatemeh Sakshat Shri Raja Lakshmi
Sakshat Shri Lakshmi-Vishnu Sakshat
Shri Adi Shakti Mataji
Shri Nirmala Devyai Namo Namaha...

Shanti Shanti Shantihi

A Self-Realized Coffee Cup

It all started in Milano, when I went for supper with my former husband and one of his colleagues. It was November, 1997. We dined in a pizzeria and as is the custom in Italy after a good meal, we took our espresso. My husband's colleague, Marina, was a young woman and was very friendly. She asked me to read the bottom of her coffee cup, as one might read tea-leaves to garner meaning about the future. I told her that I didn't believe in such things and I thought it was just play. She insisted, until I finally agreed to look into her cup. I took the small little white cup that was sitting upside down for more than ten minutes, time necessary for coffee grains to leave their trace on the walls of the cup, and started to read it. I explained:

"I see a group of people walking up toward a hill in pajamas and on top of the hill there is a very powerful, kind woman with a long stick in her hand, loose hair, and a white robe. I don't know who she is and what they are doing on top of the hill in pajamas." (1)

Marina was listening carefully; she seemed fascinated by what I was saying. At the end, I began to apologize to her for not being able to get anything about her private life or about what she wanted to hear for her future life with her boyfriend.

She thanked me and said, "Please do not apologize at all! You said the truth! For that, I would like to invite you to a meeting on Thursday at seven pm. You know, I generally don't talk about these meetings and my ideas to anyone, but it looks like you both have to come!" She never explained to us what the meeting was about, but out of courtesy, my husband and I accepted the invitation to attend. Later on, I understood that invitation was made by the Divine. God uses all tools to capture our attention, even something as simple as a little cup.

In that period of my life, I was in mourning for the loss of one of my best friends, Zhaleh. She had died of cancer in Canada, leaving three children and a husband behind. I couldn't accept that she was gone and my desire for things in life were losing color, even the desire to live. This was very strange for a person like me, who had always stood up for life and justice.

Having grown up in Iran as a tiny girl of lower class status, I was surrounded by many injustices. From a young age I decided to take a serious position of fighting against everything *not fair*, including God's rules. This presently applied to my feelings about losing Zhaleh, and how cruel life can seem.

Despite my melancholy state of mind, my husband and I went to the public program that Laura had invited us to on a foggy and cold night in November. I was attracted to all those Indian-Italian sweets. Considering the cold and damp weather of Milano in the wintertime, those were the most satisfactory things I remember.

Laura came and asked me to sit in front of her and

did something behind my back. At some point, I felt a cool breeze coming out of my neck. I turned my head back, wondering why they turned on the A.C. in winter, but there was no A.C., it was my vibrations talking. She invited me to sit quietly and not to move. I did so, and in the depths of my heart, I felt this would have been a good practice for my friend who passed away of cancer. Maybe this could have cured her. At the meeting there were different pendants of Shri Mataji on the table. One of them captured my eye and I wanted to wear it. I felt that it was giving me a sort of peace and security that I really needed at that time. In this way I got my self -realization and started to attend meetings.

My friend Zhaleh came into my dream that first night. She asked for the pendant of Mother on my neck. I kindly refused to give it to her, telling her, "You know that I'd give up even my life for you, but let me keep this and I will bring another one for you." At my return, my dear friend Zhaleh was gone. I knew then that she was at peace, and that I could also move forward in peace, with the Divine guidance of Shri Mataji.

(1) The pajamas I refer to it were in fact kurta and Panjabis, but at the time, I didn't know!

Wisdom from a Tree

I was pretty upset when I came out of the meditation center. So many little things were disturbing me: indigestible vitamin B was blowing up my stomach, blasted cold air from the A.C. on the first warm day, and people who didn't come to the program and didn't even let us know that they were not attending. So I ran to the porch in the backyard to find some refuge.

I was looking at people coming and going with their cars. The very gentle sky captured my attention. Only in that moment did I notice a huge tree with all its beautiful leaves and branches above my head.

"Hi," I said.

She answered, "Hi , what's up?"

I replied with another question: "How can you handle all this silly nonsense of life? I am so ashamed of my disturbances by so many little things, especially when I am aware of bigger problems. How do you do it?"

She said, "I am more than two hundred years old. In this little yard, I assist many of the coming and going lives, from animals to humans, and spirits. I have learned to watch them. You have to know that in this yard so many people were in love and have kissed each other lying on my trunk. So many fights I have seen with my senses, even crimes. I have felt all kinds of emotions in my veins and I have learned over the years not to keep them inside. Every emotion, the nice or ugly ones, can kill you inside or can teach you something for a better life. I decided to live and not to perish, so with each occasion I expressed myself with a new branch on my body. In order to do that I had to go deeper within my roots to provide nourishment, the sap, and become strong enough to hold together all that is around me."

I continued, amused, "So how can you recognize the bad emotions from the good ones?

"There are no more bad or good ones, as all together they create this dignified and majestic body. Bad and good are blended together to make my trunk, my life, and all the people who contributed to that are living inside this life of mine. They were merely opportunities to learn and go deeper into my roots in my contact with the Mother Earth. Now I am here to share it with you, only because you asked me. I can give you all kinds of answers because I learned to be available and generous, but you have to make your own experience. Don't be afraid or frustrated, those are the other names of death. Reach for life and make everything good for your growth!

Go to Mother! Go home!"

Om Twamewa Sakshat
Shri Shiva-Parvathi Sakshat Shri Sita
Rama Sakshat Shri Jagadamba Durga
Mata Jagadamba Sakshat Shri Adi
Shakti Mataji
Shri Nirmala Devyai Namo Namaha...

Italy, the Land of Love

After the revolution of 1979, Iranian university students were considered the most dangerous enemies for the new government. After I was rejected for the third time from my university in Tehran where I was studying my third year of foreign languages, I understood that there was no hope for me to return back to that place again. Later on I discovered that I couldn't get a job either. I was on the so called *black list* of the government of Iran. It meant that I couldn't do anything, even breathing could be denied to me. I felt like a bird in a cage. In spite of all the pressure from my parents and family members, I decided to leave the country. Until the airplane departure, I wasn't sure I would make it out alive. I know today that I was really lucky, because in those days, there were so many students and young people who were murdered or put in jail for nothing.

In September 1984 I arrived in Italy, the land of Leonardo Da Vinci and Michelangelo, my platonic loves. They were my references for life and its real values at that time. Through all my research about them, I felt deep gratitude for what they represented to humanity: the synthesis of art and science, the symbol of a new era of Homo Sapiens, the embodiment of human renaissance. They were my lanterns of hope in that world of total darkness.

Once I arrived in Italy, I decided to go immediately to

the University Admissions Department and then to the Enrollment Office for Architecture. There happened a funny accident that makes me laugh even today just to think about it. I arrived on a Saturday in Milano. In my country, Saturday is the first working day, but in Italy it is a weekend day and naturally all universities are closed. I remember that I was knocking at the tall, old fashioned wooden doors of the university with my bare hands, wondering why they didn't have any doorbell or a knob on those massive things! A man who saw my insistence came closer and asked me what I was doing there and I explained to him with my poor Italian that I was a student of *Politecnico di Milano*, and wanted to get more information about my enrollment and date of admission. He patiently explained to me that on Saturday and Sunday the university was closed and that I had to return back on Monday. I remember him repeating the word Monday, *Lunedi,* many times to get his point across.

Thus, I had the whole day in front of me to get familiar with my surroundings. I went to a nearby urban pocket park in front of the university, a round green space that was called Piazza Leonardo Da Vinci. I saw a statute of a distinct man standing in front of me on a stone stand. I thought he was Leonardo Da Vinci in modern clothing! In Iran, the statues of celebrities are located in places that carry their names, so I assumed this was Da Vinci. I attributed those modern outfits of Leonardo to Italian artistic taste! I was so happy to be in that Promised Land that I couldn't control my tears and I remember that I thanked him for accepting me to be in his presence and for all his heavenly goodness to make me become an architect. Later on, I learned that the statute was in fact a depiction of the founder of the Polytechnic University of Milan. I eventually would meet *my* Leonardo with his four students in Piazza Scala, all of them with their proper Renaissance outfits. I felt a bit embarrassed looking into his eyes on that tall stand in Piazza Scala in front of the most prominent theater in Milano, Teatro della Scala. I visited that monument many times, trying, somehow, to get to know him better.

Time passed. When I was in my third year of university in Milano, I met my first husband, Alberto. After a while, as his first act of manhood, this only son of an Italian mother came to knock at my apartment door and never turned back to his mom from that point on. His mother, Annamaria, was a rich *signora* of Milan and also the only daughter of her family. This signora did everything economically possible for her son to provide him with a comfortable life. She tried so hard to compensate for the missing space of her husband who left them when Alberto was five years old.

Our connection started with a party at his house that was close to my student dorm, Casa dello Studente. I was invited through a common friend. I was twenty-seven years old and he was twenty-three. At the party, everybody wanted to know about Iran and what was going on with the Islamic regime and the war between Iran and Iraq. Alberto came to me with a non-alcoholic cocktail in his hand and asked me how old I was. I took the glass and answered his question by half-joking that I was forty-seven. Amazingly he believed me. I didn't know if I should have felt offended or to have some tenderness toward his naiveté. Later on, in our married life, I used to tease him by reminding him of this episode. Later that night, he captured my attention with his abilities on the computer screen, showing me the freedom of making colors and lines so easily and so fast! For me that was magic and this man also appeared to me to be magical. We exchanged phone numbers the very same night.

The first time Alberto came to visit me was at the house of Mrs. Gornati, an eighty-year old lady who had hired me as her caregiver. I would go to her house every night from seven until seven the next morning. For this service that was limited to sleeping in her house in case she needed some medical assistance, I was paid 250 mille lire a month and free meals. That salary was about $120 and allowed me to pay my entire university fees and other expenses. Also, I got free grant money from the university for my good grades. With that extra money, I bought all the equipment I needed for hiking and mountain climbing. I was ready now to claim my status as a free soul who was following her dreams.

Mrs. Gornati was from a high class in status and culture and was very helpful to my studies. She assisted me with all those complex Italian literature and architectural words. Unfortunately, she got sick after a few years and I had to find an apartment on my own. One of my best friends, Grazia, a post office employee and a talented artist, left her apartment to me. That was in Via Monte Nero where Alberto had followed me.

Alberto and I loved to drive around listening to pop music: Paul McCartney, Michael Jackson, and our favorite: Depeche Mode. Our souls would fly far from our little car with the rhythm of the music. I took care of him like a little baby: cutting his nails, brushing his hair, and for the yearly festive carnivals which are celebrated vigorously in whole land of Italy, I would do his makeup. For these, Alberto generally used to wear feminine outfits, and I have to confess that in those occasions, he became a nice woman with his long legs and lashes (for one day, just for fun!).

Alberto was taking care of me in different ways also. He was very kind and humble, contrary to many Italian men I had encountered who were mostly exuberant, arrogant, and macho. He was also different than me in every sense. He was slow in his ways and that helped me to reduce my speed. He made me feel like I was living in an oasis of natural beauty in that hectic city of Milan.

At first, I worked in a Persian carpet shop, repairing damaged carpets. I learned the art of carpet repairing in the Bazaar of Tehran before leaving Iran for Italy in 1984. My work place was close to a metro station called Cadorna. In that station, no matter what, everybody was in a hurry by default, and this frantic attitude was contagious. For a young foreign girl that was out of her normal life, that rushing was not good at all. One day, my heart started aching. I felt it was from the hectic pace of that metro station, so I ceased working at the carpet shop. Later on, I got a part time job as a designer in the Sergio Coppola Studio. Alberto was an employee in a hardware computer firm and he loved it. Our jobs provided us with enough money to sustain our common life together in our small flat.

On Thursday nights, we would hang out with friends. We all met in Piazza Partigiani, very close to the Lambrate train station. This place was close to all our friend's homes. Each week, there were twenty to thirty of us standing in that square for long hours conversing. At some point, we would go to Locale, a favorite café, to spend the rest of the night together. We used to have dinner and play board games. Monopoly was our favorite one.

Yet after a while my Iranian spirit called me; to me, hanging out with friends had meant to spend time in nature, going for walks, or mountain climbing. I started to show intolerance for those long chats, eating in noisy locales, and playing games. It felt like a waste of time. I was happy for Alberto, but after a while the noise and the smoke that accumulated in those places simply made me sick. Alberto and our friends were very caring about this problem and they all tried to choose open spaces for our gatherings. I tried my best to tolerate their culture of chattering, making jokes, and smoking. I was continuously trying to understand him from my heart, even in those moments of his excitement at daily funny stories of life (which I just didn't understand!).

These friends seemed to me to be grown up children and they were so proud to express it openly: *Yes, we will never be grownups!* They decided to be anti-conformist, against the rules of their middle and high class families and society. I began to see them as a whole bunch of fluffy pink partisans of the new era, meeting in that Partisans Square to enjoy their own diversity.

After six years of studying architecture, the day of my graduation arrived. We found at the steps of our house a huge flower arrangement sent from my uncle from Germany to congratulate me. Now, we were facing a new situation. By graduating, I couldn't stay in Italy, because I wasn't a student any longer. In fact, I needed to return back to Iran. Alberto started panicking and for the first time on his clean face, I could see the signs of worry. "We have to get married." With this phrase, Alberto gave me a gold ring with stars carved on it. Since my youngest sister was getting married in one month and I had to go in Iran for her wedding, we decided to make our wedding ceremony before that.

With Silvana, my friend and university classmate, I went downtown to shop for my dress. We searched the whole of Corso Buenos Aires and found everything we needed in one day. I ended up with the perfect Jackie O. 60's style canary yellow dress and artistic high heel shoes. Yellow was my color, after all, and I looked beautiful. The last touches, a hat and a bouquet of wildflowers, completed my wedding-day ensemble.

The night before the wedding, as an Italian custom, I had to stay at my friend's house to avoid the groom seeing me before the promised day. Not only that, but I also I had to go out with girlfriends to experience my last night of freedom as a single woman.

On the day of the wedding, though I was overjoyed, when I stepped out of the Renault 4, my friend's car, I felt a tear in my heart: my parents weren't there, especially my dad who was supposed to walk me into my new life. I felt some comfort knowing I had invited my uncle and his wife from Germany to take the place of my parents at the wedding.

On July 18, 1990, forty people attended our civil marriage in the municipality building of Pieve Emanuele. The mayor officiated the ceremony and offered champagne and roses to all our guests. Our best friends, Silvana and Fabrizio, were our witnesses. It was a very simple, but gracious ceremony. I felt like a beautiful canary flying toward the sky of happiness. I was finally with my sweet other half.

Of the forty people, my mother in law, who was paying for the ceremony, decided that only twenty of them could stay for lunch. I chose a ristorante close to our house. We cut a cake in the courtyard of the restaurant, cheered with champagne, and went inside for lunch.

Alberto had decorated our modest car, "Uno," with flowers. My uncle and his wife offered us money for our honeymoon, and we set off. Together, we travelled all around Italy in our little car. Alberto made it easy to travel by creatively constructing a portable bed inside Uno. With this method, we never had to book a hotel and could travel any time we wanted to.

This was such a huge transformation for Alberto, who used to stay in five star hotels for his vacations. With me, instead, he transformed into a free spirit and he became the king of this new dimension. Every day, we woke up in a new place, with the sea as our balcony. We often stayed close to the water element, where Alberto could stay in the water fishing the whole day long. Playing and doing all kinds of water sports made him feel as if he was in paradise. We often had fish soup made of very small colorful fish he caught and patiently cleaned. He'd cook it in a pot of water with onion and lemon juice. I initially had compassion for the small fish and didn't want to eat the soup. But because of my new husband's enthusiasm, this turned out to be our best food ever to enjoy.

For that tenderness that Alberto conveyed to my soul, I started to make peace with myself and my country. He wasn't really a religious man, but faithful to God. His infinite fantasy of life and other planets and creatures were so inviting. I learned to look at life with his eyes and started to believe in God's existence. Later on I recognized Shri Mataji as the incarnation of Mother Mary, again under Alberto's influence.

On one trip, we stayed in a campsite that gave me a good opportunity to read a book entitled: *The Advent,* by Gregoire de Kalbermatten. The first half of the book was about issues around the world and how Shri Mataji was envisioning them. This was good guidance for my thirsty intellect. The second half was about metaphysics and demonstrations of God's existence. I finished the book at the rising of the sun and when I closed it, I felt a rush of excitement created by a new vision: God may exist! With that phrase I had to run out of our tent. Alberto was sleeping like a baby and I couldn't wake him. So I ran toward the sea for miles and repeated to myself: *I found it!* The scenery was so dramatic and emotional. It came to me how Archimedes might have felt under his skin, shouting out: "*I FOUND IT.*" I had gone to Italy to survive, and to search for my love. First I found myself, and then God.

* * *

Over the years, everything was not always pleasant. Alberto tried to have more comfort on these spartan vacations and added things like a tent on top of the car. The more things he added, the more I felt the need to have a warm shower and a regular bathroom.

Alberto was a good swimmer and used to go underwater with a snorkel to fish. He wanted to be at the beach from early April until the end of October. I couldn't swim and couldn't handle the hot sun on top of my head. I always had a thick book to read or study and an umbrella to block the sun.

At some point I began to work more and Alberto started to go on vacation with friends. That was the starting point of our separation, first in spirit, and then in physicality. I needed him to be close to me in those deadline moments of my work, and he began to choose the company of other people rather than me.

Soon I began to work more for a better family status and hoped to have a child. Alberto showed his refusal by increasing his time away with friends. He believed that I wouldn't be able to take care of children, because I wouldn't sacrifice a good night's sleep, which would mean he would have to! There was also his fear of the child arriving with some sickness or disorder. Despite all these fears, I did become pregnant and I watched him change. He was happy and caring, as he used to be, with no fear at all.

Unfortunately, when in my fourth month of pregnancy, I lost the twins I was carrying. My life was at risk, but Alberto did not support me. Instead, he was critical and unkind. Afterward, I was so lost and depressed that I decided to leave our home in the winter time, knowing that we were not living a dignified life together.

I stayed for a while in my downtown office in Navigli. That wasn't a good idea, because I started to build up more anger against him. After four months, he called me and asked me to come back home, but it was too late for me. I became a business monster and he closed himself in defensive walls. Soon after, we divorced.

Mother, after making sure that I could afford life economically, authorized us to divorce. She told me: "You are aware that you are no longer a young woman," and for the first time I saw that She was not pleased with me. Despite our ending, when I look back, I feel so grateful for what Alberto did for me: He helped me make peace with myself, to become part of the Sahaj family, and to retrieve my dignity by being at Her lotus feet.

Shiny as the Heart

Once upon a time,
A friend came to visit his old, dear friend.

He noticed a very beautiful red pin shining on the shirt of his companion. He couldn't understand why his friend was wearing such a precious jewel on a very common shirt, and why he was so attracted to that small shiny thing.

On the way back to his home, he saw the dew shining on a blade of grass.

The reflection of the sun's rays made the small drop shine like a diamond. He understood then that it was not the pin, but the warm heart of his friend that had made the small object so precious and brilliant.

This made his attention raise, his eyes lightening, his heart illuminated with joy.

Silently, he thanked his friend and continued on.

Andiamo per una Farinata: Let's go for a Chickpea Flatbread

Everybody knows that Italy is a synonym for good food. The fact is that Italians feel that their country is the best in everything and they really mean it. Italians love their language to the point that they rarely speak other foreign languages. They are so proud of their country that it is difficult for me to believe that they accepted to be part of European Union. However, Italy is the land of grace and open hearted people, as Shri Mataji always told us. Their kindness is so contagious that it makes one also kind.

One of the very simple, though popular, foods in Italy is *farinata*, chickpea flatbreads.These became so part of our precious moments of life together that when Alberto was asking me to make a wish for Easter, the first thing that came out of my mouth was: *Andiamo per una farinata*! We used to drive for at least two hours to go to the Liguria area to wait in a long line in a tiny, crowded, family-managed restaurant just to have a big round tray of farinata as well as other doughy delicacies: focaccia, pizza, and panzerotti. Food is a way of life in Italy.

Years later, I recall the first night that we arrived in Milan with my parents to take care of their Italian green cards. I booked two rooms in a hotel in via Ripamonti, close to my house.

After check-in, my mother stayed in the hotel and I took my father to a very famous restaurant that specialized in Sardinian cuisine. The place was very simple, nothing fancy, and felt like a restaurant for the fishermen of Sardinia. It was noisy and small with fishing nets hanging on the white walls, full of spider webs. Amazingly, to eat there you had to book in advance. The reason was simple, the good quality of the food. Furthermore, they made you pay for everything you consumed or utilized, at high cost: to begin with, that big loaf of crunchy bread and olive oil, to the hard cotton tablecloth! There was no menu; a little lady with black hair came to the table to let you know the list of the dishes of the night in a Sardinian accent. You had to go with your intuition, and even though she was so kind, as were all the staff and owners of the restaurant, their serious faces told you to hurry up. As a matter of fact there was always a long wait list and many people pushing each other at the tiny entrance of the restaurant to enter and to wait their turn.

My father and I waited for a while outside, but since my father was in his eighties, I nudged him inside, close to the counter of dead fish and live crabs, claws closed with strong elastic bands. He was enjoying them; he always enjoyed watching and eating fish of any kind. I pushed myself to another counter where the satisfied people have to wait to pay and go home with their stomachs full of bread and fish. I asked the owner, a tiny man in his 60's, "How long will we have to wait? My daddy can't stand for so long." He asked me, "Did you book?" When I told him no, he replied: "Then I am sorry, we cannot serve you, you have to reserve beforehand. As you see there is a long list of people who are trying their fortune." I was so surprised, I couldn't believe that they had become so popular in these years of economic crisis. I told him that my father comes from so far and he loves fish. We decided to wait for few minutes and just see.

I turned back to my dad, telling him that I was so sorry, I tried to book, but for tonight it was full, and did he mind going somewhere else? My father looked around himself with his shiny avid eyes, and while we were trying to guess the names of the fish on the back counter, the owner called me! He said, "I can't see your father standing this long, so go to the table…" and there was the little lady to guide us. We sat down and the waitress began to name all kinds of first and second course meals. I knew that my father doesn't take wine. So, I tried choosing something sensible, not like last year when we came to the same restaurant with my cousin and wasted 200 euros on food. Not having the menu, I went by intuition, for me only a first course and for my daddy both first and second. During the waiting time we enjoyed big crunchy bread and olive oil. Even the precious and tasty crumbles were picked up to finish in our mouth.

After just half of my meal, I began to feel full and

tired, so I thought of the American style of taking a doggy bag. In Italy this nice habit doesn't exist. In Italy one eats and elegantly leaves what they can't finish on the table. Italians generally don't reheat food, especially pastas. I had to find some justification to take home the rest of my delicious meal. I explained, "You see, my mother is in the hotel and she couldn't come because she was so tired, do you mind giving me these leftovers for her?" The lady server immediately answered, "I don't know. I have to ask." I was a little bit embarrassed, but decided to stand for it. Otherwise I would have just re-ordered the same dish to take home to my mother. I waited and waited for my father to finish all the mounds of food he was enjoying, dipping his bread in the juicy sauce. At the end I ordered a coffee for me and a dessert for him. I went to pay for our food and amazingly they made me pay relatively cheaper than what it should have been, maybe around 70 Euro, and I felt that they were so touched with my family situation. They may have thought: *Old daddy and mommy from far came to visit her and she is doing her best to please them.* I didn't feel any sense of pity from their part in that situation, just kindness. Even when they called me on my way out of the restaurant to give me a huge aluminum box with warm food, again I was a little bit embarrassed, but I felt their heart and it wasn't offensive to me. In that box to my surprise, they put not my leftovers, but a new dish, much more elaborate and rich than the one my father and I had, and they didn't even ask me to pay for it! I took it as a gift from our Mother; I was in the planet of hearts and not judgement. And of course, my sleepy mother enjoyed that food tremendously.

When Resignation Becomes Resurrection

Haideh, an Iranian pub singer was performing on my car stereo: *A dove had a baby, wish you could see; in our yard, jasmines are blooming, wish you could see...* The rhythm and words were so heartening. I blasted the car with high volume, singing with her: *...wish you could see!*

I was returning home from Cabella in Italy where I had a visit with Shri Mataji. I have never had the experience of that amount of vibrations in my blood, penetrating my bones. Only music can transmute that level of excitement before you explode.

I went there to visit Her with a very decisive attitude and with no flowers in my hand, to add a pinch of dryness. Yes that's it, I would resign and give back all the documentation and apologize for not being able to complete the job for Her. I was in charge of Mother's villa in Genova. Pressed firmly under my arm I carried the huge file of remodeling plans for the villa, a reconstruction of the garden, property border, and parking area.

I used to behave as an ordinary architect, technically patterned, with lots of ego. I remember in that period I was feeling so disturbed by Italian macho attitudes. Considering that most Italian men didn't listen to me or perhaps I didn't know how to manage them properly, I decided to resign from my task. I went to Cabella and entered Mother's castle with a strong decision to quit. I waited in the dining room, surrounded by high class colorful plates, paintings, Persian carpets, and more. Spring was depicted on the curtains, and outside the sun was singing his glory with sharp contrast of light and shadows on the roofs and trees. All this stylish mixture of culture and beauty couldn't change my idea: I would resign from my architect duty and would be free from all those Italian men that had no respect for a woman, especially if she is a foreigner and their manager. I was so fed up by their arrogance and not being respectful with the schedule! Not having any flower, as I usually did, for me was the sign of determination in my final decision. I didn't want to tell Her anything negative, that the very first job delegated from Her to someone else was not working. Under Her direction, it was assumed that everybody knew their duty and behaved themselves, but with me as a director, I didn't see any chance to overcome this situation: a voluntary position that was not traditionally coded nor ruled by customized contract. As I awaited my meeting, somebody there noticed my impatience, and began to chat over tea about different topics, trying to distract me. Yet I couldn't even hear her voice; I didn't want to lose the momentum of my frustration and final decision.

Finally, I was called in. She received me in Her bedroom. Her bed was so beautiful and very well arranged, always with a love that goes beyond any style and exactitude. She sat in front of me on a Her puffy red chair, on the right side of Her bed. It was just me with Her in that bedroom filled with beautiful fragrant flowers. I did Namaskar and didn't even wait to hear, "God bless you!" before raising my head in a sign of my determination for what I was going to do. When I looked at Her big glowing eyes, I felt so transparent that I couldn't hide anything. I said to myself, *She knows why I am here*, and that helped me to relax a bit. The first thing She asked me was: "So how are you?"

"I am OK Mother," I replied.

"So how do you feel?" She continued. The same response came out of me. I began to have some hesitation of this last answer: is She referring to me and my recent separation or the job that was assigned to me?

To cover my confusion, I started by saying: "Here, I brought all the files and documents of your villa..."

Before finishing my sentence, She said, "Oh my God, you did all this?"

I kept myself steady enough to resist my softening heart and with a strong voice replied: "It's nothing Mother, they were done two years ago." I meant to express that there had been no progress in two years.

She immediately commented: "But you did a lot."

In that very moment I saw her beautiful eyes shine bright tears. Even a stone couldn't resist melting all that perceived drama. Seeing Her eyes wet, my heart opened and I understood that it was about a job for *Her*, and nobody else mattered in that task.

We chatted for some time, touching different topics, during which She didn't stop praising me, calming down my huge, wounded ego. By this time, I knew I would continue to work on this project. I was amazed how we could understand each other beyond any language barrier.

With my head bent, I asked if She was going to ask for permits for another building.

When I heard "Yes," I immediately asked when I would have to start? I had just overcome the overwhelm of one project, would I so soon have to undertake another one? It was clear to me that I had changed my will and attitude too fast and that it wasn't me, but my inner conscious that was indulging to know about everything now. And I knew that it meant more trouble on the way! Maybe She heard these silent words in my head and comforted me by saying, "I don't know, it's better that my son in-law takes care of it, if he wants that place. But let's finish this one first!" I thanked God for that response.

Next She asked me about my ex-husband, expressing Her sorrow for what happened between us. I tried to explain that he was a good person, but not a responsible husband in our life together. She told me that her assistant hadn't told Her all the truth when she was preparing to find me a match, so now She was going to match me with an Indian architect. I turned back to my senses and felt as though I was talking to my own mother, and so replied in a daughterly tone: "No Mother, please, don't. Otherwise when we fight may kill each other by throwing bricks against one another!" She laughed hard.

Then She asked me why I didn't go to stay in Genova, where my jobsite was? I knew that for some strange reason I couldn't really handle that city. I explained that in two years my house would be out of contract and that now I was going to London to visit one of my friends and to better learn the English language so that I could speak more easily with Her. She limited her response to say: "So, I will be with you." And this became true. From that day forward she was truly with me in all ways.

Mother asked about my work and how I managed such a masculine job: It should be difficult for a tiny Iranian woman to be an architect in Italy, shouldn't it? I confirmed and explained: "You know these Italians are basically taught not to take professional women seriously." Then all of a sudden if the men were inclined to take sympathy on these women, they become so kind. At that point they open the gates of good possibilities to them that men can't ever access.

With that habitual wonder of mine, I went further and told Her about one of my episodes in municipality. I had been waiting a long time for the mayor of Milan to arrive so I could ask for a permit for a green village. Finally, his assistant received us. My male colleague and I entered his office and from the beginning he never gave me any respect worthy of attention. Since the idea of that project was mine and I wanted to arrive at some resolution and have more clarity, I continued to ask questions, as was my habitual way of understanding what to do next.

The assistant ignored me again and again, and in that snobbish attitude of people in power, directed his response to my colleague: "We Italians understand these things immediately, but for *them*," signaling me with his head, "It's so difficult to get it." He continued by asking my colleague where I was from.

Those days, they were blasting the news all over the country, with Bin Laden's action platform in Afghanistan, and the hellish Taliban, poverty and war were immediately associated with that country (and still are). Some devilish force in me took the tragedy at hand and began to play a sarcastic act: "I am from Afghanistan, and for us it is so easy to resolve problems with a bomb in hand. We don't need to be intelligent or even discuss the situation..." I joked, referring to the terrorist mentality. The assistant immediately got the subtlety of my joke. After that moment, he changed his arrogant attitude toward me and answered all my questions!

At the very end of our meeting, in a sarcastic way, he joked: "Now that you got the information needed, please keep this building untouched."

My response was immediate. "I will talk to my highers…and *will see*." We both smiled with an understanding of what brought us to that dry humor. My colleague was astonished and couldn't understand what was going on. He spent time with his mouth open in wonder, his head moving like a ping-pong ball from me to the mayor's assistant, back and forth. The fact is that this funny man signed all permits for us with no objections toward such a project.

As I recounted this story, Mother was listening to me with such attention; there was some deep understanding and complicity beyond the language barrier between us. The moment was filled with lots of wonder and laughter. She lauded me with so many beautiful words that I have already forgotten, surely soothing for the ego. I just remember that three times She repeated this sentence: "I will be with you!"

Once out of Her room, I was embracing life in all its glory. The windshield of my old Ford Fiesta was filled with colorful trees pouring joy from the sky and God's melody was blasting in my interiors. Jasmines were blooming inside my heart.

I turned back home knowing that She knew about everything. I talked to the major Sahaj contactor about the desire of Mother to finish the job before the expiry date of the building permit. As always, he showed me his disapproval by saying that I wasn't good enough to manage the job. Before my meeting with Mother, such behavior would bother me quite a bit, but now I was beyond any disturbance! My response to him was, "Ok. Well, you are good enough and you are going to help me to finish it, right? I was a different person. I was shocked by the power of Her sweetness in us and Her ability to penetrate us to get the job done: the job of becoming better humans!

Silent Passing of the Years

I was in Ocean City, Maryland. I invited my friend's mother, who came from overseas to visit her daughter, for lunch. I had shared lots of adventures with this friend and we often talked over a cup of tea or on the phone. It's so nice to know there is always somebody thinking about you and that you can take somebody in your heart everywhere, whether travelling or doing errands. We would often chat in the evenings to share the highlights of our days and to have each other's opinions about silly or important things. When we were on the phone, nobody could disturb us; it was such a sacred time that they would know to have respect for it.

So, it was obvious that I would want to have her mother in our house. The bell rang and I rushed to open the door. I greeted my friend, her husband and children, but couldn't see her mother. Instead, there appeared to be her older sister in front of me. I asked about her mom and her sister replied, "Here I am."

I was sort of shocked: "Are you? How could it be? You look younger than me!" In saying these words, I began to recognize that come to think of it, my friend never dyed her hair to cover the gray, nor did she ever complain of joint pain. Yet she had been my friend in equality. I began to recognize that she was always so respectful to me, but that could be in any friendship in which one friend is wiser, so what? And finally, I got it: I am as old or even older than her mother! In our relationship, we had never questioned or been concerned with how old we were.

This episode helped me to see my position better, not as an older woman, that's implied, but of how souls can go beyond any limitations. Sharing life, enjoying life, living, has no boundaries and this reality is possible for us through the light of Spirit. Again, through the light of Spirit we can forget about our physicality and life stages. So my friend, our ages do not matter, what is important is what we do together in cherishing our Spirit. Thank you for being my friend. If this old age made me wiser, I love it; if it helps me to be the friend of younger people, I am happy. I learned from this experience that a friend is a gift from God and you don't need to analyze it.

Divine Justice

The positive aspects of being in Italy are not unknown to me. I know the people and their culture. I am familiar with the way they make exaggerated expressions as a way of hiding their emotions, or the way they use sarcasm to make fun of themselves. Generally speaking, Italians are kind and warm, and truly, one can feel the good influence of an ancient culture in the people's daily life and attitudes. For example, if a neighbor for some reason hides himself or is sad or worried, you can be sure that an indulging Italian, especially from southern part of Italy, will appear at his doorstep with a cup of coffee, a good excuse to make him talk!

It's true that when trouble starts, it will be one after another. After months of living in the US, I had to return to Italy to take care of my studio and apartment which I had learned was being occupied by squatters. The turmoil I had to go through from afar was unbearable. At one point, I was even ready to give up; to leave my house in the hands of those invaders, but my husband reminded me that it was not right; that I should go there and fight for my rights in a detached way. Surely there was an opportunity for me to grow.

The prospect of talking to one of my tenants face to face was creating a bit of anxiety for me. I had to say, this man's transformation into a mischievous fellow was not all his own fault. In Italy, the remnants of an ex-socialist government created the general mindset that only cunning people could take advantage of and exploit the already corrupt system. Those who enter Italy illegally are aware that shelter, food, and some salary is always waiting for them. Certain exploitative organizations and many mafia associations have learned how to cleanse their money by recycling it through charities or donationations. There are far reaching fellows who use their money in partnership with some legal advocates to control all of the human traffic and illegal immigrants in and out of their county.

My tenant Surya was one of them. Surya was a poor, socially marginalized man from Sri Lanka who tried his luck by coming in Italy in open waters. Many immigrants are "hired" by some phantasmal company and then are sent to jobs based on the provinces and places from whence they came. Those from Sri Lanka, called *Chingalesis*, took the very common in appearance, but sensitive job of concierge or door guardians. These doormen would often have all the building affairs under control; they would know exactly who was coming and going, who each tenant was, and which elder people might need extra support. In this way, the mafia or other corrupt bosses would have their eyes and ears inside the whole building, infesting it like so many termites. Their well-organized networking systems took advantage of those situations where people couldn't be at home regularly or perhaps had some economic problem handling fees and taxes. Foreigners like Surya were modern slaves of a confused system that only fed the corruption and opportunism. Knowing this, coupled with all of the inner changes in myself since I had left Italy helped me to stay calm and see the greater picture. As I prepared for this task I said to myself, *I surrender!*

On the first night of my arrival, I slept at the house of Nail, my ex-cleaning lady who had become a friend. I couldn't sleep thinking of the next day and what would happen. If God, with His compassion in his witness state treats all humans the same way, He may not provide the fair justice on my side and send the squatters away. I really wasn't sure how the justice of God may be expressed in these complex situations where desperate people are occupying a house that belongs to somebody else who doesn't live there. There was such a noisy battle inside me; I questioned my values, my mistakes, and my worthiness. Only around four o'clock in the morning, I felt Her protection, Her benevolence showering upon me, so soon after that I finally felt still and could sleep for few hours. Now I knew I could let it go by, no matter which kind of result this life was reserving for me. I felt the divine play and my role in it: *just play the game!*

The next morning, I faced Surya, my former tenant, who now was in my house unlawfully. We were both respectful to each other. He promised me that he would leave the apartment, based on a court verdict, on time. That was more than enough for me for that day.

In the late afternoon, I took the train to Cabella where I could stay in Castle Doria that belonged to Shri Mataji. Two hours later, I jumped on the bed of the beautiful second-level shared room in the castle. I don't remember how long I slept, but it didn't matter to know, as I was truly in heaven!

The following day I was back in Milano, spying on the front door of my studio from the opposite side of the street. Behind me was a green area belonging to the *Parco Sud*, a park of the southern part of Milan and former agricultural area. This section was not quite a hinterland, but was isolated enough. The long street of *Via Ripamonti* becomes the main vein of connection between downtown and the exits to the main highway connections. My apartment and studio were located in this peaceful part of the city. There one can still find parking and easily take a long walk in pure nature. From this point runs one of the most important canals of the city, belonging to the main hospital called *Ospedale Maggiore*, the Great Hospital. Maybe the presence of the canal was the reason for all that precious greenery present in the otherwise dense city of Milan.

I was feeling the cool six o'clock morning breeze coming from the park behind me. The studio at the first floor was connected to the apartment located at the second floor, for my own comfort. I had to separate these two properties to rent them individually. I had rented the apartment to a family with two children and the studio after a while was rented to a young girl from Sri Lanka. Those crooked people were recommended by a well-paid realtor who later had her office burned down, either by accident or let's say by the wrath of Hanumana.

There was no movement from my studio. I felt like a detective in an American movie.

Finally, at seven, I decided to go knock on the door. A dark, tiny man, a so called cousin, appeared at the door, telling me that he spoke with my tenant who had been in her distant country of Sri Lanka for several months. He assured me that she wanted to pay the rent and invited me to be more patient. This did not sit well with me. It was clear I was being deceived.

At that point I decided to ask for the help of police officers. To my surprise they told me that even though my tenant was not at home, her guest had the right to be there and that I couldn't do anything about it. But I wasn't there to hear their stories and rules; I wanted my studio back at any cost. I decided to return after a few days with Enzo, my friend's husband, and meanwhile I could spend some time with my visiting parents in Cabella at Castle Doria.

Several days later, in the company of Enzo, I knocked on the door of my apartment in Milano again, and a lady came out with wet hair, telling us that the signora, the landlady, wasn't at home. I explained to her that this wasn't a home, but a studio, and that I was the landlady. I clarified that her signora was in fact just a tenant, that she was not even paying rent, and that I was going to take my studio back from them. She replied that she (and the tiny man from the days before) were going for a trip and that their baggage was ready to be loaded into the car as soon as their friend arrived.

Meanwhile, they were calling somebody. The car came with a distinct man at the driver's seat, who suggested that I lock everything up while these tenants were gone. But, immediately after this friendly talk, another "cousin" called Sisil came, and the woman passed the studio keys to him before I could grasp them from her. The cousin was so tempered and had such an authority about him. I tried to threaten him by calling the police and asked him to show me his ID to see if he was really a cousin of hers. The moment he showed me the ID, I grasped it. Sisil tried to take it back by straining my wrist. The driver told him something in their language, so he let me go with his ID. I was shivering at the shock of such an assault. Nobody, even Enzo, couldn't help me. Later, he told me that no woman could have done that. Enzo was also under shock. I felt that I had reached the depths of my fears. This violence was beyond my expectation. I had the experience of Mother's will and deeds again. Some malevolent and ugly people had actually helped to switch the situation.

There is an Iranian saying: If God wants, your enemy will cause your good luck. In forcing my hand to his ID back, Sisil had sprained my wrist, which gave me a reason to get to the hospital and then to the police office. When the police eventually came to my studio, they found lots of illegal people's documents in the house. This ultimately lead to the officers removing Sisil, an illegal immigrant, from my studio as well.

Nail, along with my friend Gianna, came to help me with taking photos of the squatters' belongings in the studio, making a list of them and transferring everything into my basement.

Now I was ready to face the court judgment (which is generally in tenants' and squatters' favor, again because of the corruption and misinterpretation of socialism in that country). And meanwhile I installed the strongest locks for my studio.

Soon after, my friend's teenage daughter Elena came to stay with me. After that ordeal, I was so grateful to have any breathing being beside me. Elena naturally wanted to have fun and eat good food. It was good therapy for me to remove my attention from all that ugliness to an energetic teenager's needs. After taking care of Elena's desires and curiosity for a big city, I again called the police to settle the matter once and for all. While I had cleared out my studio, I was still unable to access the upstairs apartment. When the police arrived, I showed them the original agreement of my tenant Surya to vacate the apartment by early August.

The police had to go up from the studio side and forcefully kick out the wall created between the studio and apartment. The two officers who did it were refined and strong men; I was surprised by their determination and force. I felt compassion rising in me and humbled about my harsh judgment against Italy and its authorities. They both got their realization afterward.

The scene of these two huge men sitting in my little studio with their guns released, saying:

Mother please come to my heart was so dramatic.

After that, I could then close the entrance door to the studio with a metal bar, and this way block any access to the apartment from outside. The scene of Surya's return and inability to enter the apartment was better than any action film. He tried and tried, nervously. He called out and ran up and down the street like a crazy man. I was watching this from the gas station in front of the building. Finally, he got the tram and left the place.

Later on we called him to come to pick up his staff. What was surprising for me was that the building's cleaning man was from the same country of my former tenant. He confided in me that they had been friends and that he knew one day this would happen that he would be kicked out. Discreetly, and almost with fear, he helped me to carry the tenant's personal items down to the first floor. Surya arrived two days later in the early morning with two others. One was an aggressive friend who pretended to be his lawyer, and tried to force the door open with tools.

At that point I had to yet again call the police. The

collective atmosphere at that period of time in history was so scary. When I described that two foreigners were trying to force the door to enter in my apartment, the authorities immediately thought it may be a terrorist attack! They even asked me the stature of the men and how big they were, their approximate ages and their nationality before coming. Those three men pretended that my tenant had his passport inside and he had to go in to get it. I knew this trick of entering and then again occupying the place. I refused. I was left by myself, even my angel friend Gianna refused to be with me. She was outside in the parking lot inside her car, watching this drama. I was shaking and scared and the police officers over the phone couldn't calm me down. This got worse when one of the prostitutes of that building offered them better tools to break the lock.

When the police arrived, I once again felt the support of the Italian authorities more than ever. They hushed those men and as the "lawyer" questioned their protection of me, a foreigner (forgetting that he too was an immigrant), the officers answered: "She may be a foreigner, but a very respectful one. She is an architect who has worked here for so many years." Those words and titles sounded like *amrita* to my soul. For the very first time, my title and my character was publicly appreciated!

While this episode provided temporary relief, I am sorry to say that the situation did not end there. I had to leave for a brief time, and when I returned, I learned that a former tenant had found access to the upstairs apartment via a staircase that I thought had been sufficiently blocked.

I went to meet with my first floor tenant, Surya, who had agreed to move out in a few weeks, but he didn't show up. Instead, I found a strange man sleeping inside the studio with the windows open. I called him, but there was no reaction. I thought he maybe was dead, considering that his big belly didn't move up and down. I then picked up a long stick, and through the iron grates of the window, pushed his tummy. He finally reacted and came to open the door for me.

Here was another illegal person who had residency in my apartment!

I entered the apartment, attempting to scare the intrusive pot-bellied man. Soon Surya arrived and I realized that since there was no way for me to physically get them out of the door, I had to try another tactic and engage in the divine play. I managed to get Surya to sign an agreement letter to leave the apartment earlier than the court had requested, in late July.

It was now June and I thought that I would have to wait until my next trip to Italy to finally be rid of these tenants once and for all. Yet destiny had another plan: I was able to enter the house and lock it from the inside with a huge log. In keeping my faith and benevolence, which I learned from Shri Rama, I had the dignity and strength to hold the situation together and remain lucid while doing so.

To finally complete the scenario, I needed to change the locks to be sure nobody could enter the apartment after I left. When I arrived at the door of the key shop, the owner couldn't help me that much. He continued to explain, "It's almost noon, everybody is at lunch now... and then they all my handymen are heading out to work for the afternoon." There was a young customer who was paying for some items and I looked at him with a glowing eye: Can you please help me? I understood that in moments of real need, humans (myself included) can push beyond any border of shamelessness.

I discovered that this kind soul was a designer and carpenter and he offered to come to my apartment with his little red car. A real perfect Italian man, finally! He not only changed the locks in no time, but also helped me to remove the nasty mats leftover from my tenant. I couldn't help myself, with eyes filled with tears and I gave him a big hug. I offered this kind man one hundred Euro for his time but he refused, saying, "You called me your angel for today, so how could you pay your angel?"

I was in a total wonder. Something fantastic was happening. After all of this drama I wondered if maybe one had to rely on emergency situations to see the good nature of Italians? I have no answer to this question even after all these years. I know that Italians have good hearts despite living in a system corrupted by lust, greed, and immorality. By the end of that apartment debacle,

I felt overwhelmed by all of the "bad" and "good" people involved; it had been such a battle! Yet I was left feeling that miracles are truly made of the most ordinary occurrences.

At that time I had been reading the Ramayana, huge in its content. I began to feel in my bones the story of a perfect man, Shri Rama. How much he and his beloved had to go through with no complaints. They knew it was a test and that they had to surrender to their destiny. Even the people who I was dealing with, those squatters I had struggled to expel from my apartment, were from the same land of *Lanka* where the Ramayana took place. As a result of all this, I began to have more and more awareness about what was going on. The fact was that I had become stronger and gained more dignity. I learned to be kind to everybody around me.

Memories from Cabella

My American husband and I had arrived in Italy less than a month ago. We missed the shuttle of Malpensa-Cabella and decided to go with an Italian friend to her house for lunch. We had pasta con ragu, chicken, salad, dessert, and coffee. An ordinary Italian meal.

After lunch I was so excited to go to check my studio in Milan. During my last visit to Italy, less than one year prior, it had been transformed into a Sahaj Center. The vibrations made it more beautiful than ever! Gunter, an Austrian yogi years younger than me had painted trompe l'oeil scenes on all the walls, inspired by Tuscan landscapes. The second floor was painted to look like a wooden ceiling with hanging bunches of Lilacs; they looked so natural that it felt as though I could almost smell their fragrances! Everything was so inviting that we decided to stay there for the night.

The day after, we were on our way to Cabella in the car of a senior yogini. It had been at least five years since I had spoken to her. We limited our relationship to some emails once in a while, and now in her car we had at least an hour to talk. She told me about her experience after Mother's departure: "In the living room of the castle with Mother's body displayed for the last goodbye...She was so beautiful, smiling, and relaxed." She felt that for an instance Mother moved one of Her eyelids. She told me how she was thrilled and couldn't believe what she saw, but when another yogini saw the same thing, she began to accept it as a divine message.

From the very first moment of our arrival to the main door of Mother's castle, I felt something magical in the air. I knew that place very well, and made namaskar in front of Her door. The tall wooden door was filled, as always, with all kinds of flowers of different colors and fragrances. One could feel the emanation of blessings floating in the air, a scent of giving and receiving love was glittering on each petal of those colorful flowers. It was the best welcome I have ever received in my life!

I went in search of Marianna, the volunteer coordinator of the castle, but to my wonder the castle was deserted. I led my husband to the men's room downstairs, where the year prior, my father got a bed. After setting his bed and baggage, I went to the ladies' room upstairs, where last year my mother and I slept. The ceiling of that room was my passion: a huge brown dome, with bunches of white roses hanging down in all their glory and full expression of health and fragrance. Along with them there were different pinkish roses and beyond that other colorful flowers. I could feel their generous caress telling me: "Hey you are here again, feel yourself at home and enjoy your life with us!" Every morning I could hear them saying, "*Buon giorno!*" wishing me a beautiful day, and every single night a warm, "*Buona notte! Dormi bene,*" leading me to have a good sleep. It was so encouraging to start and finish my day as a volunteer at the castle of Shri Mataji in that way.

The yoginis in my room were of different countries and ages. I knew Elena, an Italian lady who was living in the castle with her son. I used to call her "*la cavalla selvaggia,*" the wild horse: a friendly, passionate, and autonomous lady. She was an artisan, working on mosaics for the back door panels of the castle. Elena was available to everyone, with words of immense knowledge or with preparation of a mud pack for an injured leg. When I first met her in the village of Genoa, even though we had little occasion to talk, I immediately felt her to be a good friend.

Two other young ladies were Silvina, twenty-four, who won the first prize of a short film contest led by the then Prime Minister Tony Blair, and the other was Brenda, a twenty-nine year old actress that had starred in Silvana's film. They were both from Argentina and came to Cabella for Adi Shakti Puja and to run a new project, a new film! Silvina, who was an ex-model and a university graduate, changed her career to filmmaking after getting her realization. She was so humble and beautifully simple. She told me about her father, her family, and her relationships, as did her friend Brenda. Brenda was also a script writer. She loved to act as a clown too. That magical concept, *clown,* had always been something so interesting to me. It seemed the best way to go directly to the heart of people, even for our

Sahaja programs. A clown is an innocent personality that everybody can relate to with ease.

We got used to talking a lot, even into the night, especially when Silvina left the castle for another destination. Brenda told me how after realization, her life was changed. Even though she had lost everything: fame, money, country, parents, friends, and was now living like a vagabond, not knowing what or where her next steps would be, she was sure in her heart that was the way it had to be. She felt that Mother was with her always and that she was on the right path. Her only question was, "Why? Why do we have to go through all of this?!" I felt so much similarity between our lives and so began to tell her my favorite story: Krishna and the Goat. Her big green eyes began to open wider and softer, only quietly commenting, "Oh," as I told the tale. By the end, we both held tears of being honored by following our destiny. Yes, behind this apparent cruelty was the compassion of God. Together we recognized how lucky we were! Not race, not age, no apparent difference of any kind could intrude in our unity. In that special moment, in that room, those roses on the ceiling were the only ones to celebrate the bond of our sistership.

Kitchen. Such a deep word. That year I had to be the chef for twenty-five people. It is some mysterious effect on people hearing that there is someone from Iran that they assume that person will cook well. Automatically, I was praised with this title of so much responsibility.

The first thing I did before I began my chef experience was to pray to Mother deeply in my heart: "Please let me remember how to do *risotto alla Milanese!"* After so many years of abstinence, Mother really helped me, and the result was more than satisfactory.

The second day I made *pasta al pesto*, and it was so delicious to my palette, but I discovered that most of the people didn't like the main ingredient: the spaghetti! The third day I tried an Iranian dish, struggling with a lack of the necessary main ingredients. To my protest, Marianna told me: "Be Sahaj, use your fantasy!" God saved me this time too- I made a beautiful dish of rice, yellow lentils, chicken, and onion. My yogi brothers and sisters always loved what I cooked, firstly because they are kind and forgiving and then of course there were the vibrations of Mother's castle. On the fourth day, I made a huge salad with delicious ingredients unusual for an ordinary salad. I decided to be successful at the cost of over doing it with the ingredients. It was so exciting every day to have the challenge of satisfying the yogis, coming with such appetites after their morning duties.

The curious sisters who wanted to learn all the culinary secrets were always creating stimulating and playful moments. It would not be honest if I didn't admit that I was often stupidly worried about the timing and the results of these meals, but one can imagine that. We even invented a "cocktail" using leeks as straws for drinking. When everything was ready, one had to make the most glorious announcement: *E' pronto*- It's ready, and in the glance of an eye there were so many yogis in line with their metallic plates, cups, and huge pieces of watermelon in hand. Every day we would taste a different herbal tea crafted by experts; I had never heard so many Latin words, as the yogis referred to the different teas. Seperate from the challenging vocabulary of those tiny delicate herbs, the real nature of each was in their taste and fragrances: smooth and relaxing. There were different herbs for different problems, but in drinking them we never paid attention to that, we were just happy to enjoy them together.

Most of us loved to eat at the small table in the kitchen of the *mezzanino* by putting the chairs closer to each other. Two doors away was the meditation room with bigger tables for consuming our food. Maybe because of the presence of Mother on the opposite wall, we couldn't feel comfortable talking and making a mess as we used to in the kitchen! Our daily breakfast was the most relevant meal of day. Every morning we received two big packs of fifty breads of different shapes & tastes (*michette*, *tartarughe*, *franceschini*, bagels, etc). The aroma of those hot fresh breads stimulated our hunger. We'd cut the bread, then put a big layer of butter and large spoonful of jam or honey and enjoy with a cup of tea or orzo (a coffee substitute made with roasted oats), and milk. At the end, we'd close our bountiful breakfast with an Italian tradition of espresso. For me, breakfast was the most important meal, and I usually chose healthier foods.

But at this time, I truly enjoyed our "unhealthy" start. For two weeks, it was a real treat that I never would've permitted myself at home!

* * *

In my twenty-one years in Italy, I graduated from the architectural university and ran my own business, got married and then divorced; all of these were just part of my personal experiences of life. I met a lot of people and made so many friends. Nowadays, I generally don't tell everybody that I am going to Italy; otherwise I would have to spend all my time with visiting rituals. So, I choose one family or friend to see each time. One particular time, I asked my dear friend Silvana, who was familiar with Sahaj and received her realization years ago, to come to visit me in Cabella.

We met at Mother's castle, and she looked so different from the young Silvana I had met years back. She, with her husband and two sons, stayed at Hotel Bruno, close to the castle. Gianna, another friend that occasionally meditated, got a room at the house of one of the Sahaja yoginis. First they were invited to meditate with us in the living room of Mother (such a treat!), and then we took them to the waterfall in the high hills at the back of the castle. We enjoyed the cold water and the scenery of the white rocks lying still under the crystalline running water. Naturally, it turned out to be a school of nature for those two little boys. At the end of the day, the boys and all of my friends didn't want to leave. We promised each other to do the same thing in my next visit to Italy.

It was routine for all yogis go to the mezzanine every morning at eight-thirty and every evening at nine. In a very spontaneous way, some of us could guide the meditations and put on a video of Mother. Otherwise, we all stayed in a silent meditation. That silence, mixed with the vibrations, and the birds' chirping, was so powerful! In the morning one could decorate and clean the altar as was their pleasure, and one day I felt I had my chance. To touch Her feet and face with the soft cotton and rosewater transported me immediately to Sahasrara and I could see how simple and natural elements, especially flowers, could express such an emanation of love and respect in different ways, but always so beautiful: it was the magic of our Mother!

Then there was the opportunity to go to Her living room on weekends for meditation. Wow. There in that room, where I stayed at Her feet so many times to discuss Her house and other matters… I could hear Her chatters, jokes, stories, and laugher, all mixed together like musical notes, to create waves of wisdom around me. Only my tears could clap with appreciation to that Divine symphony! I was sitting in front of Her photo, her large smile inviting me to come closer as she used to do in life. My first human reaction was the one of an upset child: *Oh Mother why have you left us?* To that question the response was a strong flow of vibrations, so strong that they washed away everything, including my sadness and filled me with a huge amount of joy. I felt a profound respect and gratitude expressed from those Sahaja yogis who came from different places just to be there, as they called it, Heaven. I was almost drunk and so foggy that I wasn't sure if I could remember how to meditate! I was sitting at the exact point where She used to put Her feet, and where all yogis around the world came to see Her in peaceful silence for the very last time at Her funeral. I couldn't bring myself to be present for the funeral, but in that moment I could feel that pouring of her love upon Her children while the whole cosmos was holding its breath: Adi Shakti had left the earth.

At the top left of the wall, a photo of Mother with Her husband, who was holding Her hand in his with such respect and sweetness, made me turn back to my physical body by drying my running tears. I left that majestic room to take refuge in my daily and familiar life.

In my free time I used to go to my favorite place on the creek. It is not such a popular point, because it takes a long walk along a dark tall wall, behind the *Bar Italia*. At the very end there was a house of the former city representative, a sweet old lady who had already passed away. Her house was my preferred one in Cabella, so much that I was thinking that it would be wonderful to live there and to travel to Milan every morning to reach my studio. This house was made with a mixture of Italian and English style. There was a main house with a beautiful sunroom. In the middle of the yard, there was another little house for guests. In the front part was a pond with a statue of a little boy sitting at the top of a fountain, and further there was a pergola of kiwi plants hanging down. Under the pergola was a stone table with varied wooden benches. Everything was so lovely and naturally beautiful. All was a testimony of artistic and joyful taste. Behind the side wall of the house was a stream running down from the far mountains. This house was so blessed with all surrounding elements, it was truly a place to cherish.

Farther down the stream is a huge, flat, stone bed that you can use for your sunbath.

Down the stony wall is a creek divided into three branches. I used to stay by the one closest to the wall. Sitting there on a stone with my feet in the water, I used to chat with little fish and rocks around my feet. Every single time, I watched the curves of the hills and greenery of the village in front of me, with the sun shining directly into my face, and thanked the sky, the air, and the birds for letting me be there to stay with them: Thank you Mother!

Om Twamewa Sakshat

Shri Radha-Krishna Sakshat Shri Adi Shakti Mataji
Shri Nirmala Devyai Namo Namaha...

My Life in the USA with Steven

Have you ever been in a very down state of moodiness? How many times do so many of us go through depressive moments? I was in one of those moments when my husband switched on a TV comic show. There I got a special message for me!

A man said to his brother: "Your research of finding who you are is not outside. That is the reason you couldn't ever find it." The other man had been so busy helping other people instead of the closest person to him, his brother. Toward the end, he recognized that the purpose of his life was not so far away, but close. His brother got the assistance he had been silently begging for and he got the satisfaction of being of assistance to his brother. Both were happy.

Life is so simple, if we are innocent enough to see through the manipulations of the mind. Everything is there ready for us to get done, without doing!

When I read my diary of my past experiences, especially with men, I recognize the huge gaps in my writing, or in other words, the lack of reflection. Today however, reading those memories doesn't engage me much. It feels like reading about another person. I see how twenty years of my life sheds like the papery layer of an onion.

I graduated in Italy, got married for the first time in Italy, worked and opened my architectural studio in

Milan, divorced there and bought a house there, but the most important event in Italy was that I met my spiritual Mother, my Master and my Goddess. Could these intense experiences have happened anywhere else, but Italy?

Going even further back in time, I see how God saved me from Iran, softened my Iranian pride and cultivated the assertiveness of a business woman, bringing up those Lakshmi qualities in me. I gained my dignity drop by drop after going through all those experiences, surviving and returning. All this was only because of the support of Sandra Karuna.

In the USA, it was time to live life fully based on past experiences. For this I had to make right culture. I thought that maybe with my second husband I would be able to go through this. I sensed that this time it was not only about me, but *us*. Only together we could reach the high waves of happiness and serenity. I needed to be kind with myself and also with others to fulfill this mission!

We were in Virginia Beach and I was in front of a big window that serves as a live screen to the scenery of the wild ocean, along with the sky, and the birds making an excellent play of fantastic drama for their audience. I had left behind lots of confusion and delusions: Ending a job at a big department store, sufferance caused by my tenants in Italy, mental pressure from social problems in Iran, and the death of my dear Uncle Mohamad. Even more, my two younger sisters, Nahid and Parvin, started to fight with each other, a yogi I knew got cancer and a yogini friend had lost her child. In addition, some important events happened. The Sahaj center of Frederick, Maryland was started in August 2008, after an exhausting discussion to get the approval from our local council. Obama was the president of the United States of America, and we celebrated the eightieth birthday of my daddy in Germany.

From all of these trials and experiences, I learned to be humble, and not to do things for the sake of making others happy. It was time to look inward at the cost of feeling selfish. I recall years ago in Genoa when Mother Mataji put her hands on my head and asked me to make a wish; I immediately wished to be a good yogini and to reach that stage where I am conscious about the amount of work I have in front of me. Time is short and my way is long!

Outside it was becoming dark and I needed to go out and purify myself (*ghosl* in the Persian language). What better occasion to trust the love within to lead? To make all this digging inside stronger, I had a big mirror which covered one of the walls where I would sit. It reminded me of my childhood on Shahbaz Street; we had a huge basement and a little tiny mirror there. I used to go to this mirror every single day at different times to talk, comment, and plan my future. Now, I could see that little girl again, questioning her best friend, her reflection: *Could you ever imagine ending up here?* Soon after that, a gush of gratitude covered my body, I was full of wonder at how far I had come along under the skin of life.

I had recently finished a queen size comforter quilt for Mother, with the Kundalini all made up of colorful flowers. Nights before I had a dream that a very young and beautiful Shri Mataji was at the door of one of the yoginis, but the woman closed the door in Her face very rudely with lots of complaints. Mother was wondering in Her compassion. I wondered, *Was that about me?* Was I living not in happiness, but dryness? Had I missed the point? It felt as though at times I had been moving through life like a bulldozer, all the while forgetting my joy, losing sight of the reason I was doing any of it. To leave the best Guest outside the door of my home, my heart! How stupidly I could push myself in that wrong direction. I believed that I needed more deep diving in the pure water to remove all of these thoughts and open the door for more wisdom, thoughtlessness, and purity as did our Lord Christ.

Years ago, an Italian friend that is a rare honest man wrote me a letter in which he described me as stubborn, critical, intelligent, arrogant, and with a savior attitude. When I hear his words today, I think of how exigent and assertive I was and how my expectations could bring out all the best of a person, along with the sufferance of facing the truth about ourselves. My husband Steven is the one that surpasses all those expectations in comprehension, strength, and determination. I believe that after all life experiences, I am able to appreciate him the most and the best. He is always there for me in every situation, accepting me for what, who, and how I am. He pays my bills, but mostly he loves me.

Steven and I live a routine life of getting up late, meditating, eating, taking a walk, working on a list of projects together, watching some movies together, and again meditating before going to bed late.

To my benefit, I am learning to accept him as he accepts me. I enjoy and admire Steven's being slow, indulgent, dramatic and talkative. I've had an intense life for my age and my status. Living on three different continents made me understand that God wants me to get to some resolution soon. All those years have brought me here at the present moment. It is good to consider the past, but to be alert of the present is more important, because it is here where we ascend.

Chatting with Mr. Crow

I was desperate, there was a thunderstorm developing in my heart. My new home in the US had me feeling homesick, I had no job, was struggling to learn a new language, and take care of a new home, all while getting to know my new husband Steven.

The sky outside was like my heart, cloudy and dark, ready to shed tears, expressing deep sadness and confusion inside. It was as if nature was with me, understanding me completely. The storm even shed some drops over my face to let me know its existence. I took refuge under a nearby gazebo.

In that moment I felt the wind moving the branches, it was telling me, *I am here too*. Divine scenery was acting on the stage. Birds widely opened their wings as a sign of unity between us, they were a bridge between humans and the sky; I could read and hear those messages with an inner wisdom talking to me.

I sat down under the dome, the center point of the gazebo, and listened with questions in my head: *What do I have to do? Why is it so difficult? How…* I couldn't finish my thoughts, for the sun appeared for an instant to give me a kiss, just for a fraction of a second, and then again it was cloudy and crying with my pain. Despite the storm, there was such a harmony around me. The only disturbance was the rough, insisting call of a crow.

After a while I had to bring my attention back from

that harmonious symphony to its noisy indulgent call. I asked him, "Yes? What's the matter with you?" The crow replied. "I just wanted to tell you that those evil thoughts want to push you down!" "So what? Like I don't know about all these trials and interferences." I told it with nervousness in my voice.

Then the crow, with its eyes full of love, replied, "I know that you know; I am here to remind you that 2012 is so close and the battle of ego and superego is at the last stage. If you don't go beyond these two false powers, it is your END. Do you remember in Cabella? How everything was so gracefully different? How you were able to stay balanced so easily? With no agenda still everything was flowing so smoothly in tune with all. Do you remember?"

"Yes!" I answered, hesitating. "But which one is reality?"

"The only one that gives you joy, the one that keeps your heart beating regularly, the one which made you thoughtlessly aware, the one that takes care of you with good food and good sleep, because your heart is worth cherishing," the crow replied.

"Ok, Ok! Stop now! I don't need your preaching, I know all this in my heart, but how is it that I am so worthy and still so heavy inside at the same time?"

"You are so worthy because you could see Her, touch Her, speak with Her, and have some memories of Her, which only has to be enough for living gratefully! But in desperation or low mood you are not able to give the right value to the right things. I came to remove your darkness and remind you of the truth. You could have been dead years ago. Even before your realization, She took care of you. You could be lost in your limited mind or be so badly sick, but now you are able to appreciate fireflies, can talk to the trees, can run with the flowing water of the creek, and most of all can feel the Divine vibrations.

Now, because of all these powers with you and around you, you have entered in the real battle of the last judgment! You are Her soldier! The worst of the worst enemies has entered in your mind. No one can recognize these enemies without purity, courage, and dedication. It takes years to master it. You may be old for a regular life, but you are so young for a spiritual life, and this is a *spiritual* battle in a *regular* life. It is not easy, believe me, to live with all these dualities. Just hang in there and watch with trust in your heart that She is always with you! Just watch and obey."

I was lost in those words and can't remember when the crow stopped talking. I was so absorbed in my understanding that everything around me was showing me this union with Her, even if I am not aware of it. Nature is always with us, helping us to perform Her work. Only we have to have courage and humility to go forward saying, "Your kingdom come, Thy will be done..."

I promised myself not to give any more nourishment to the negative forces. I said goodbye to the gazebo, the sky, the crow, and the whole of nature, and turned back home again, understanding the worth of my heart.

My Sahaj Family

I have a huge Family here in the USA. They came from different countries: Russia, India, Argentina, Columbia, Brazil, Spain, Iran, Italy, and of course the United States of America.

My Family is made of different generations: so many little children and adolescents, aunties, uncles, grandmas, and grandpas, all under the same roof. We have so many good artists, musicians, and singers in my Family. They are often so quiet and just dedicated to sing or play, but when they guide the meditation, even the youngest ones are so deep and mature.

My Family is made up of so many retirees, artists, laborers, doctors, scientists, college students, architects, caregivers, householders, doctors, managers, and more. Although there are people in my Family with all kinds of different ways of living, when you ask them, "How are you?" They smile and reply: *Jay Shri Mataji.*

My Family loves to get together for making handicrafts, sewing, painting, cooking and making special sweets. We love food and are excited to offer and share our new recipes in abundance. In my Family, generosity is unlimited regarding projects, fundraising, and group endeavors; we just make it happen.

My Family cares about our birthdays. They send the list of each month's birthdays and desire for each person the best wishes; if somebody wants to give a gift they know when the day and the right moment is. When it is the birthday of a one year old girl, they all come to say hello to the little child. My Family likes parties of any kind. For picnics, you find such a huge number that all of a sudden it becomes difficult sometimes to manage with the tables or to book a large enough space!

My Family is so patient with those who try to show off, they smile softly and listen to them, and let the melting power of love take over. Tolerance is another virtue of my Family. When somebody pushes their agenda and claims something has to be done in a determined way, they nod their heads to say, "You are right," helping the person to purge the sickness from their inflated head.

In my Family, there are so many disciplined and organized people who know how to follow the steps to get the job done, they are not afraid of knocking on the doors of some impossible institutions. We have people who are scouting non-stop in search of the best occasions and locations for our programs. There are so many who do what is asked of in humility and obedience, even though they have their own ideas of things.

Like all families, sometimes we get upset with each other and may even fight openly, but a while later, we arrive waving hands and asking, "How are you?" My Family is always there for you when you are in need: childbirth, death, and family issues.

Such a rich diverse people are in my Family and I don't ever forget those special and ordinary moments I have spent with them. All this and more is to say how much I love them and how much I feel lucky to have them! All the thanks go to our Mother for creating this Family and that string of love among us.

Krishna and the Goat

Krishna and his disciple were walking, and suddenly found it was night. They walked a while and came to a huge castle. They went in and there were received by a very powerful, important king, full of riches. That night he gave a party in his home in honor of Krishna. Many guests came to celebrate the great event. The king asked Krishna to stay the night. Krishna accepted and enjoyed the comforts of the place and its infinite delicacies. The following morning, while others were in deep sleep, he and his disciple left the castle. On the way out, close to the castle gate, Krishna looked over his shoulder and with a soft movement of his hand, blessed the king. The riches of the king increased immensely. The castle was much bigger than before, and the king was even more powerful. Krishna's disciple was wondering why his Lord did this, but said nothing.

That same night, they arrived at the house of a peasant in the middle of the field. He was a very poor man, with few tools for living. He had a tiny goat which gave them just a glass of milk for dinner to share. There was nothing else, but much love. In the early morning of the following day, before leaving, Krishna went to the goat, put his knife to its throat, and killed it. His disciple couldn't stay in silence more: "Why did you do that? Why from this poor man did you take the only thing that he had for his living, and to that king you gave everything one can imagine?" Krishna replied: "For the king, it will take him a long time to get to Me, he has time to live his plentiful life, so I gave him more to enjoy. But between Me and the peasant was only a tiny goat. He could come sooner to Me, but that little goat was a distraction, keeping him far from Reality."

Panther Cloud

I felt so tired that I decided to take a nap under a pine tree outside our door on the canal in Ocean City. As usual, I put down our thick white sheet on the grass, watching boats dangling against the wall of the canal and creating circles on the calm muddy water of the bay. Everything was rippling toward the bay, even the sky. I turned my head to look at the mouth of the bay where everything was swallowed into it. The reflection of the sky was so alive and inviting. I raised my head to look above and I noticed a huge winged white panther cloud.

Before I could close my open mouth, he flew toward me and before I could escape, he swallowed me with his gaping jaws. I could feel the watery air on my skin and the comfortable puffiness of it. But the most important thing is that I was flying over the bay with no mechanical or electronic device; wherever I glanced, I was there. I was soaring over the bay and the ocean, on or in that huge puffy panther. I started to breathe steadily and asked with a shaking voice in the air: "Who is this? What do you want from me?"

Even though I was amazingly happy inside, I tried to find the way back home, thinking that was the way to be safe. I was struggling between my childish bubbling heart and the joy of flying, and my grown up reasoning that I should be at home with my husband and family, inventing all kinds of reasons to return back. Somehow though, my glances couldn't touch the direction.

Om Twamewa Sakshat
Shri Jesus-Mary Mata Sakshat Shri
Maha Ganesha Sakshat Shri Adi Shakti
Mataji
Shri Nirmala Devyai Namo Namaha...

Poems for Her

Try to Be

"Cercare di essere" is a common saying in Italy.
They recognize the way to survive through the dangerous games of life.
I know the path of joy has always been there for us;
It is us that must try to walk on it and to dig into it:
Under the skin of life is only joy.
I am grateful.
In love with life.
Living in the wind.
Flying with the wind.
I am the wind.
On the green hills I stay
Under a sanctuary in clay
Into the river,
Stopping behind a rock,
Staring at a new stem of algae on the white calcites of the bridge,
I stay and watch
The cascades of light mixed with dews,
I caress the grains of sand in my mouth.
I swallow life in all its aspects
I stay,

I watch
I exist, not lost!

I Asked and She Answered

I asked: From which city did you buy your wisdom?
She answered: From experience!
I asked: From which flower did you get the tenderness of this fragrance?
She answered: From experience!
I asked: From which candle did you steal the gaze of your eyes?
She answered: From experience!
I asked: From from where did you obtain your purity, simplicity, warmth of heart, and being a witness?
She answered: From experience!
I asked: From where have all these blessings come?
She answered: From experience!

Her Bindi

Warm pulsation of the earth,
Slow down my breath!
Fragrance of flowers on the air,
Fill all my expanded cells!
The chirping of the birds stop,
As a melody plays inside...
All floating, alert!
All expand in softness!
"She is coming..."
my heart whispers!
Behind that mountain shape of joined hands,
Above those closed eyes.
She is watching me!
She is a rising round velvet sun!
She is there!
Toward the inside, in eternal contemplation,
Closed eyes...
Through that globe of light...
She is watching universes!
She is watching us!
She is watching me!
In that state of being part of the whole...
No more fear!
No more..., no more...,
Rising in totality...
Beyond the formless shapes...
Touching the essence...

Where the silence seals,
Her Bindi reveals!
"The Oneness" is...
Her Bindi!

A Blade of Grass

I put my mind at Your feet
I put my heart at Your feet
My body
My emotions and thoughts,
Everything is Yours,
Everything I surrender at Your feet,
Now...
Can I be a blade of grass under your feet?
Simple and dancing in tune with the wind,
Humble and rooted in earth,
Happy and looking up into the sun,
A simple blade of grass,
At your feet!

Baby Dolphin for Steven

A black spot out of ocean crest
Up and down in the blue sky and waves
He brings joy to everybody
Busy people stop to take a picture
His gray mommy is behind him
So subtle is her support
Denying even her existence
Soft and cautious
Behind the young dolphin is always
His majestic mom!

Mona Lisa Smile

To reach Her...
Up to the hill
Thousands of men in silent walk
With only one song of their heart beat
Down to the hill
Angels and Gods in flowing float
With the sound of cascading water
The point of the Union
Where She stands
Humans and Gods become glittering dots of
Her Robe
Lively silence!
Mona Lisa smiles

***The Fragrance of Spring* (Inspired by a Persian Lyric)**

The cool breeze of your Feet
Fragrance of spring
Blossoming of your Face
Fragrance of spring
The pleats of Your sari
Hyacinth clusters are
On Your shoulder Mother
Fragrance of spring
Such fresh jasmine flowers
I had never seen in my life
That white of your throat
Fragrance of spring
You're the dove of our temple
Your songs at early dawn
Bring truth, peace, and joy!
Fragrance of spring
Laughing fish are in your eyes
Your Bindi crowns our praise
And our meditations
Fragrance of spring
In my heart have been always
Nothing but autumns
The paradise of your desire
Fragrance of spring
Fragrance of spring
Fragrance of spring

There is More...

Once upon the time
I had a dream
We the people of the world
We, Her creation
We were One!
In peace and understanding
In joy of sharing
I had this dream
For a long time
She came and told me
There is more
Imagine...
You are all singing my name
From North Pole to the South Pole
In all continents
In all colors and languages
At the feet of the Himalayas
In Sahasrara and Lagoons together
Under the waters, in the air
Imagine all of a sudden
The sky opens
And all the angels and Gods
Make the chorus higher
With the same melody
All together
To dance
Earth and Heaven dance

Imagine my heart
Full of bliss
As a lotus opens
Petal after petal
To embrace you all
Showering my love
Melting you in me and me in you
Until becoming One
Imagine nothing but
The silence of Love!
The Silence...

We Are

This morning I woke up
With the load concert of birds,
So melodious and joy giving that
I couldn't get up even for my daily meditation!
It seems the doors of heaven
Suddenly are opened by a magical force.
Almost all day that concert affected my life
By removing all the obstacles
And reminding me of Rumi:
All religions, all this singing, one song.
The differences are just
Illusion and vanity.
The sun's light looks a little different
on this wall than it does on that wall.
And a lot different on this other one
But it is still one light.
We have borrowed these clothes,
these time and personalities,
from the light.
And when we praise,
we're pouring them back in!

Listen

Listen under the noise, talks, TV and AC.
Listen to the tree and her growing roots, the soil and her busy worms
Listen into the dew on a blade of grass that saw a white flower blooming.
They can tell you about the joy of this newborn with no name.
Listen over the lightened candle that tells you how wonderful is the support of Mr. Wax.
Listen beyond the air blowing...
Wow how much news is running around the world?
Ducks and geese going to the North, a little wren preparing another nest,
a hawk caught a mouse on Route 15.
Listen to the sky and cloud community: Today a dark one called Sad Blu was set free.
Listen to the butterfly: the palpitation in her flying is not because of confusion,
but of amazement in her short five hours of life.
Listen to the Vibrations all around you, your life, your heart...
There are lots of spaces, gaps, resurrections inside them.
Listen to the Sun: be brave in listening.
Do not watch in his gaze. He will teach you how to burn obstacles inside.

We gain strength with our listening,
No waste and no heat into the ether, light, wind, water, earth elements,
Just Listen!
Listening makes me kinder to myself, makes me have peace with myself.
How many good things have I done, that I am not aware of?
What about the bad things?
They are there only to give more color to my woven frame of life.
How many experiences, challenges, or ideas have made up this root of mine?
Listening softens my being,
Enables me to follow the melody of my destiny in a dance...
To create, to give and to accept
To be available without any prejudice
To suffer with the awareness that it's part of my evolving.
Listen to the sensation of peace inside.
Listen to the thrilling enchantment of counting your blessings.
Listen beyond this or that of your mind.
Listen to the music of silence, the joy sprouting from it.
Listen to the formless God inside you, beyond sensations.
Listen to the silence of surrender
Listen!

A Dialogue with Rumi

No mirror ever became iron again No bread
ever became wheat
No ripened grape ever became sour fruit
Mature yourself and secure from
a change for worse. Become light.

- Rumi

To reflect my fragility, I had to become as strong as
iron again
To nourish more than bread, I am learning
to become a wheat sprout
For the joy of variety, I show sourness to
envelop deeply the value of sweetness As the
path of growth, maturity never ends,
We just go round around on a spiral scale
Hoping one day to reach Her Bindi again
and again

- Crazy ZoRe

Mother's Eyes

Darts of light,
Your beautiful eyes
Upon me.
Darts of light
Pointing at my heart,
My eyes.
Everything raising my being into the
Knowledge of God.
A woman like me,
How beautiful she feels
With Your eyes inside.
Thank you Mother
For letting me love Your Eyes!
For letting me love You!

The Mother Moon

I feel my heart is ready ...
Yes I am ready to embrace your love ...
I can now rise up
Leaving behind the rest of "mine"
Black and white
Pepper and salt
Falling down...
Grab a balloon
To go higher
I see what I left behind
Higher and higher
With more confidence ...
Hanging feet touch the clouds
My arms become wings of desire
I take a breath,
Near the reddish moon
Finally I find my alcove...
Part of the moon
I am the Moon!

Om Twamewa Sakshat
Shri Kalki Sakshat
Shri Adi Shakti Mataji
Shri Nirmala Devayi Namo Namaha...

Memories of Mother

Mother asked us to sit at Her feet. We were in Genoa with Alganesh, Her Eritrean helper who we used to call Alga (1), and the contractor who would do the restoring job for Her villa. The second floor of that old villa was going to be Her floor to stay while other floors were dedicated to other functions. From the large windows of that huge stone house we could see all kinds of fruit trees and roses climbing over the ruined walls around them. In that awesome view, the whole city and the sea were under Her feet.

We sat and She put Her left hand on my head and told me to make a wish; I wished to be a good yogini and nothing else. After a while She removed Her hand from my head and told me, "Your liver is better now!" She also told Alga that I was a follower of Hazrate Fatimeh. That statement, to associate me with the Islamic world, had always disturbed me. But this time I asked Alga if I heard it right and she replied, "Yes, but She is also Mahamaya!" I made namaskar and in front of my lips found Mother's left pinky toe. The temptation was so strong that I put a kiss on that little toe. She pulled Her foot back immediately and looked at me with those big eyes in amazement. I realized later that what I did was so out of protocol and for this transgression I could have been transformed into ashes, but again in Her immense compassion, She let me go! Once out of the building,

I was craving sugar and I ran to an ice-cream shop to nourish my poor liver!

(1) After leaving behind my office as also my home, I went to live at Alga's house for more than a year. One day she came back from Cabella with a message of Mother for me: Stop thinking about injustice and suffering of women, especially Iranians, you are a yogini now! I never felt that I was thinking about this issue so ardently that Mother's attention captured it. I didn't realize it was even in my consciousness, even now, after so many years, but surely that sufferance is built into my being and Mother knew better than I did.

* * *

We were sitting with Mother in Her Dining room and she was vividly talking about here and there while we were trying to explain to Her some issues with the Her villa restorations in Genoa. All of the sudden She stopped talking and looked at me and asked, "How did you come to Italy?"

I was familiar with that question, since so many people in my almost ten years of living and working in Italy asked me frequently. At the beginning, I would try to explain everything in a glamorous way, only to find very often the same shocking feedback: people were generally superficial or non-empathic to my explanations. Their reactions were exhausting and the follow-up question was regularly, "Do you have airplanes in Iran?!" Initially this sign of pure ignorance made me feel sad. Later on I became annoyed and finally upset. As the years passed, I started using sort of a dry humor in responding to this question. "Well… first I took a donkey to get out of Tehran and then changed to different camels to reach Milan." Only the sarcasm of my response could shake people up and change the topic. At that point people tried to show their wonder about my country and to discover finally that it was not just an Arabic country nor full of barren deserts only.

Now again, I was in front of the same question with my same annoyed attitude, but I knew that I couldn't be rude or sarcastic with Her, so I simply answered, "I took an airplane!" Mother laughed and then told us about a great deal She had that day in buying beautiful porcelain statues of elephants in the open market, mercatone, at only ten Euro each. She invited us to go to another room to see them. I really didn't care about those statutes, but it was a good opportunity to get up and grab my sweater. Every time She put Her feet against us, there was such cold air coming toward us. On the way to the other room, I went to check the windows, and to my wonder, they were closed. It truly had been her Divine breeze making us so chilled. We came back and again sat in front of Her even though contrary to Duilio, I couldn't hide my dryness and showed no enthusiasm in seeing those "deals."

So again She asked me: How did you come to Italy? This time, I thought maybe She is referring to my past politically active life, but I didn't ever talk about it with Her. Or maybe She thought that I was too young to travel alone…? So in my answer I wanted to assure Her that it was not a difficult task for me, I took an airplane!

Mother again talked about other things, from being a Grammy, to Her shopping deals, and other funny stories about the political situation in the world, all with such ease and non-hesitation. I thought how it would have been nice to have had these visions and proper answers when I was struggling to figure out the world, studying hard, analyzing, discussing, and failing. She was so genuine in giving the right picture of the issues, the core of the problems for each country and the solutions for them. From Grammy, She transformed into a high caliber politician and then into a powerful Goddess and finally at the same time into a compassionate Mother. I marvelled at Her abilities of transformation and the warmth in Her eyes. At some point She stopped and again asked me, "How did you come to Italy?" This time a voice from very deep inside me answered, *You wanted me here Mother and so I came.* This time She smiled and I felt that meant that finally I got it! I felt so stupid by delaying in giving the right response. In Iran is a saying: *Dozarish oftad*, which means, she finally got it!

* * *

I was in front of Her in India. It was Christmas Puja and they called seven ladies on the stage to hold the sari for Mother. Six ladies were already there in a glance of an eye, but the seventh one was delaying. I waited and waited and finally felt that maybe I should go. In fact that was the truth!

Once there, Shri Mataji looked at me and asked me, "What are you doing here?"

I responded, "I came for Puja, Mother."

She then inquired, where were the others: "Where is Guido, why aren't the Italians here?"

I replied, "I know somebody was coming for filming, but I don't know what happened to them."

She looked upset. I told her, "I am here Mother." She then smiled and looked at me with those loving eyes, scanning me from top to toe. After Puja, I felt so much pain in my abdomen and I remember that had to spend the whole night in the bathroom wondering what I had eaten to make me so sick!

With dawn, I noticed that I was light like a feather. Hours later I was dancing on the stage. That was the very first time I learned about the penetrating and cleansing power of Her eyes. Maybe She had also cleaned the whole of Italy!

* * *

We were in Christmas Puja in 2004, sitting for a long time waiting for Mother to arrive. I was so upset that She had changed the place of the puja from the beautiful shores of Ganapatipule to this place whose name I didn't even know. The swimsuit I had brought with me had no use.

At some point, I felt the earth shaking under me and was so absorbed in my angry thoughts that I didn't give any attention to it. Again the earth shook and finally She arrived, small, sick, and old. I burst into tears. My mind was challenging me: *What are you doing here Zohreh? Look at her, is She really your guru? Look at Her, She is so sick and powerless.* My ego was teasing me and my overwhelming emotions were transformed into tears running down continuously. Another shake, and I got a grip of myself and responded: *I know, I know, but this is the place for me to be, I don't know any other place to go.* With that I was announcing my desperate choice to myself.

The day after, we learned that on the 26th of December there had been an earthquake and tsunami in the Indian Ocean with a magnitude of 9.1 - 9.3, destroying villages next to the coast. Ganapatipule beach and its small town, located twenty-five kilometers north of Ratnagiri, next to the Konkan coast of Maharashtra, could have been a real dangerous place for Her children. It was clear that this was the reason She changed the place for Puja.

Not only that, but later on I a book of memories by Linda Taylor, in which another yogini who was at the same Puja saw Mother in the same way I did: old, sick, and powerless. That yogini though had such depth of understanding of who was the Adishakti that she said to herself: *Oh Mother, I know you are not old or sick.* Only with those words, she could see the transformation of Mother into a young and beautiful Goddess. I recognized how I had played into the hands of my ego and my false perceptions to the point that I couldn't see the truth. This episode showed me how much I am slave of my own perceptions, that duality is in our head while reality sits in the heart!

Dreams

I was living temporarily in my studio after my separation. It was located at *Navigli di Mialno*, a prominent place full of cafés and restaurants around the channels of water made by Leonardo Da Vinci. I was trying to find a place to live, possibly next to my office, but it was so difficult to find the right spot during that cold November.

Navigli is a beautiful touristic area and one shouldn't feel alone at all by living or working there, but I was closing myself in more and more, like a turtle. I was sick, scared, and desperate. I used to sleep on a small table where we held our meetings. One night She came in my dream and told me, "Zohreh, do not worry, everything will be OK, you will see..." Her voice, at that very moment, transformed into the melody of a flute. I tried to understand and asked people around me in the dream what she meant, but nobody could help me, not only in the dream, but also in my waking state.

Time passed and I came to live in America, the land of Krishna, through my Sahaj wedding. It was then that I recalled the dream and mother's fluted voice. She was telling me back then to follow Krishna's melody to my destiny!

* * *

It was just before my Sahaj marriage. I wanted to go to India and submerge myself in the river Ganga; I had a sort of need for cleansing, for purifying. I had a dream of the Ganga River, immense and wavy. All of the sudden from the bubbles emerged Mother in a soft crystal dome, like a soap bubble. She was the Ganga River in human form, all transparent shiny with a white bridal gown. After a while with Her, I saw Sir C.P. arise in a black groom's suit. Sir C.P. was holding a silver plate full of medicines offered to Mother.

Immediately after this dream I was matched with Steven Marchitelli who was (and is) a physical therapist and nutritionist. He has been taking care of me with all his knowledge of different supplements and advice in these medical fields and beyond. Thank You Mother!

From Silence to Silence

At the very beginning, it was so dark and there was a huge silence, *SA*... and purity permeated every pore of that silence. The only being was a curly trunked elephant. Ganesha was holding all of creation!

The next step was the big bang. The egg of Brahma broke in two pieces: the lower piece that had to hold all, again Ganesha, and the upper one was his little brother. *OM* echoed and life began with reverberation of *RE*. After that, was the time of different species. They flipped in the water with the sound of *GA*. Water was the first element for making material beings. So the Mother, the cause of all, came to see her creation through the air, just like a bird, and told them: "Come to me, my dear darlings." She permeated her children with that caring love of a mother, and as a reflex, her children replayed *MA*.

Now was the time of Father to support all that, to give prosperity, discipline, and encouragement for the growth of his children. He said, "You are part of the whole. Come and see me in your higher state." And the children replied, *PA*. The time was ready for the little brother of Ganesha who was growing so fast. He was a very good example of how creation had to be. Issa was so forgiving, but not with everyone. So he went on to the higher level to take care of everything, including his beloveds. He decided that those who were not light filled could not pass through the gates of Heaven. He said it was necessary for evolution and for the thriving of what his Mother created, so his family and friends called him *DA*.

For those who understand the real happiness in their lives and are kind to others, there was the possibility to arrive at the shapeless dimension where no more matter, nothing but the Spirit, *NI* dwells. Finally, for those who could polish their souls of all doubts, thoughts, and worries, for those who were pure, peaceful and especially satisfied, there was again Silence, *SA*. These ones could understand that this Silence was very different from the first one, and recognize the value of its infinite spiral and ascending power.

Sakshat Shri Adi Shakti Mataji Shri Nirmala Devyai Namo Namaha

First Edition 2019
Second Edition 2020- USA
ISBN: 978-0-9978364-2-4 Peace land book
ISBN: 978-0-9978364-3-1Peace land e-book

CPSIA information can be obtained
at www.ICGtesting.com
Printed in the USA
BVHW040247201220
596067BV00007B/164

9 780997 836424